CW01158041

Written and researched by

Leonore and Olivia Dicker

Designed and illustrated by

Felio Sotomayor

www.portfelio.co.uk

Typefaces used: Gotham and Mercury

www.dontbelieveinjetlag.com

© 2014 by Don't Believe in Jet-Lag Ltd

ISBN: 978-0-9929241-1-9

All rights reserved. 1st Edition, Beirut.

THE FOOD GUIDE:
BEIRUT ON A PLATE

BEIRUT

- **A** Hamra & Clemenceau
- **B** Mar Elias
- **C** Raouche & Ain El Mreisseh & Zaitunay Bay
- **D** Downtown
- **E** Achrafieh
- **F** Monnot & Sodeco
- **G** Gemmayeh & Saifi
- **H** Mar Mikhael
- **I** Bourj Hammoud & Dora
- **J** Sin El Fil

TABLE OF CONTENTS

Acknowledgments	6
Foreword	7
Introduction	8
Shortlist	26
A weekend in Beirut: with your lover	29
with your friends	33
on a tight-ass budget	37
Reviews: Hamra & Clemenceau	43
Mar Elias	61
Raouché & Ain El Mreisseh & Zaitunay Bay	65
Downtown	75
Achrafieh	85
Monnot & Sodeco	101
Gemmayzeh & Saifi	117
Mar Mikhael	135
Bourj Hammoud and Dora	151
Sin El Fil	161
Outside Beirut: Bekaa Valley	169
Mount Lebanon	179
North	199
South	206
Guided tours	212
Tips	213
Survival Menu	216
Free translator	234
Recipes	236

ACKNOWLEDGMENTS

For our first guide, which initially seemed like an easy thing to pull off but with time revealed its true colours, we'd like to thank those who have kindly helped us along the way, through their tips, guidance and words of encouragement.

Many thanks to you guys and please go on being awesome. In no particular order, the list includes: Lyne Karam, Colette Kahil, Sako Akelian, Yousef Harati, Karim Safieddine, Felio Sotomayor, Romain Zimmermann, Uche Graves, Henri Songeur.

View on the Pigeons' Rock in Raouché (p.65)

FOREWORD

While travelling, have you ever noticed how worn out the "eat and drink" section in your guide has become, compared to the other pristine chapters? We have.

Don't Believe in Jet-Lag is a travel guide that focuses on food and drink. In these pages you'll find everything from the history behind culinary customs, to the tastiest recipes around. And of course this includes reviews of our favourite restaurants and bars, farmer's markets, food shops, and hidden delights. When it comes to food in Lebanon, we've got you covered.

For our first guide, we were craving Lebanese food, so we packed our bags, readied our appetites and moved to Beirut. Whether you're a fellow resident, a Lebanese expat, or simply passing through, we hope to awaken your inner-foodie and guide you to some delicious treats.

Well ladies and gents, that's our cue to leave you to it. We hope you will delight in every bit of this city as much as we did.

Sahtein, as they say here, or *Bon Appétit* as they say where we come from.

INTRODUCTION

A GUIDE TO BEIRUT

Welcome to Lebanon! You're probably thinking "another *Hummus* country?!". For many years, Lebanon has battled its Arab neighbours for the title of "Creator of *Hummus*". In May 2010, the Guinness Book of World Records recognised Lebanon for creating the largest dish of Hummus in the world. Prepared by 300 cooks in the village of al-Fanar, near Beirut, the massive dip weighed more than 10 tonnes! So yeah ... it is indeed another *Hummus* country.

If you're being served *Hummus*, it's usually because you ordered Mezze. For those who are unfamiliar with the term, we are referring to a selection of small cold and hot dishes that are all served at once – but don't be overwhelmed. They can be served for breakfast, lunch or dinner, and come as a starter or as a meal on its own. So dip into some delicious *Baba Ghannouj*, try their famous *Tabouleh*, have a *Falafel* or two and finish with some amazing grilled *Halloumi*. In other words have some colourful, fresh and healthy food. It's the best way to taste a bit of everything and a great example of what Lebanon itself represents.

HISTORY

Lebanon has no fewer than 18 different communities, which can be further subdivided into political and religious groups. But before politics, there's history.

It is well known that there are more Lebanese people living outside Lebanon than there are living in the country. This is mainly the result of thousands of years of occupation. Originally home to the Phoenicians, and then subsequently conquered by the Assyrians, the Persians, the Greeks, the Romans, the Arabs, the Crusaders, the Ottoman Turks and most recently the French, not to mention Lebanon's own civil war from 1975-1990, this country has some stories to tell. Its complicated history has greatly impacted its culinary evolution, as the country has borrowed delicacies from all of its colonisers. For example the Ottoman Turks, who ruled from 1516 to around 1918, introduced olive oil, fresh bread, *Laban* (popular yoghurt), *Baklawa* (popular pastry dessert), as well as stuffed vegetables and nuts, and increased the use of lamb in everyday cooking. After the Ottomans were defeated in World War I, France took control of Lebanon until 1943, when the country won its independence. During this time, the French brought some of their favourite goodies along and familiarised the Lebanese to "flan", a caramel custard dessert, and of course, their famous croissants. Since the French occupation, Beirut has earned the reputation of being the "Paris of the Middle East". The country is home to many different customs, has fed from the multiple cultures passing through, and has kept bits and pieces of its favourite recipes.

In Lebanon there is no "other". There are three main languages, so don't get confused when you hear: "Hi! Kifak! Ça va?" Your culinary experience will blend traditional dishes from the mountain villages with cutting edge contemporary cuisine found in Beirut. Funnily enough, though the region's smallest country, it offers the most complex cuisine, combining the best aspects of its culture to please every taste bud. So if not religion, ethnicity or politics, Lebanese people all share *Kibbeh*, *Labneh* and *Manouche*.

But don't start pigging out just yet, as there's still loads to come.

BREAKFAST

You won't want to start your day on an empty stomach. It's difficult to think of a Lebanese breakfast that is more craved than the *Manouche* (pronounced man-oosh-eh), a round flat bread covered with *Za'atar* (thyme, *Sumac* and sesame seeds) mixed with olive oil and baked in the oven or on top of a metal dome. Known for being the food of the poor or the best cheap eat in town (along with *Falafel*), this everyday flat-bread is so deeply rooted in the Lebanese cul-

INTRODUCTION

ture that every neighbourhood or village has at least one bakery dedicated to it. Manouche literally translates as "decorated" or "stamped", referring to how the dough is flattened with the baker's fingertips, leaving loads of prints on it.

Manouche is also known as the Lebanese pizza, with various toppings to choose from: *Akkawi* cheese, *Kishk* (dried yoghurt and Burghul), spinach, meat, eggs and Qawarma (seasoned minced lamb and pine nuts). The original and, according to many, best, is *Za'atar*, – dipping thick bread in olive oil mixed with *Za'atar* is also typical for breakfast – but we encourage you to try them all.

So grab your *Manouche* and eat it with a handful of fresh mint, tomatoes, *Labneh* and cucumber. De-lish.

For those with a sweet tooth, who don't mind eating a zillion calories all at once, another option for breakfast would be melted sweet cheese in sweet bread, also known as *Knefe* – which has less of a fatty ring to it, wouldn't you agree? Originally from Nablus in Palestine, Knefe is a layer of very fine vermicelli-like pastry (Khishnah), mixed with a semi-fluid clarified butter, called *Ghee* (which also means "fat" in Hindu), placed on top of a layer of *Akkawi* un-salted cheese and baked in a *Sidr*. The *Sidr* is displayed outside most patisseries, as the smell and *Knefe* shown in plain sight tends to attract customers. It comes in a special sesame seed sweet flatbread called *Kaak* and is then covered with sugar syrup. #Needs-to-be-eaten-on-the-spot-while-hot-and-stretchy.
That said, your lack of food self-control will doubtlessly take care of that, as you wouldn't be able to save it for later if you tried.

Some say this sweet treat is generally eaten on Sunday mornings or as a dessert, although we've witnessed the Lebanese munching on *Knefe* in the post-clubbing early morning. You will most probably see a massive queue of people up for a drunken feast at most late-night bakeries in town, as it's a good way to avoid feeling too shitty the next day. Well, in terms of hangover at least, it won't do anything to cure your food guilt. And that's just breakfast.

MARKET & MOUNEH

We all know that hard work tastes good, and because Lebanese food is so labour-intensive, lunch and dinner are often prepared shortly after breakfast. The women start by going to the Souk (market) to buy fresh ingredients from local farmers. The availability of products is subject to the rhythm of the seasons and although land is limited, Lebanon oddly manages to produce almost all of its own food using less than 30% of its land.

Food shopping in Souks isn't exclusive to upcoming meals, it's also great for Mouneh. For most Lebanese people, Mouneh evokes something homely. Not only a culinary tradition, but also a way of life. The word comes from "Mana" in Arabic, meaning to store. There used to be a time when it was prepared during the summer months to be eaten during the harsh winter days, a ritual that was crucial for peasants in remote villages. Nowadays, it has become part of the culinary heritage for some, and a way to avoid waste for others. Mouneh has different purposes but is basically used to preserve different foods, all found in markets.

Fruits are naturally sweet and juicy, mainly because Lebanon is a

Mouneh jars in Hamra's Earth Market (p.43)

warm and sunny country. So how do you keep all summer fruits for winter? Just *Mouneh* them into delicious jams, yummy marmalades and tasty syrups. Other delicacies that really stand out in markets are grains and vegetables. Clearly, you don't need to do much to conserve grains (chickpeas, beans, lentils, rice, wheat) but greens require more care and can be preserved in different ways, one of which involves soaking them in water, salt, and vinegar. Drying vegetables on a string in the sun used to be common practice; nowadays they are stored in jars with extra virgin olive oil.

Fresh herbs and plants are what give a little somethin' somethin' extra to Lebanese dishes. In order to preserve them, we recommend you dry them. Blending spices is just what people do here, like the famous *Za'atar* used for *Manouche*. It is common for Lebanese families to have their own secret combination of seven spices.

The blend is, to its creators, a source of pride and a distinguishing element. You don't mess with someone's seven spices! This could include allspice, cinnamon, clove, ginger, black pepper, nutmeg and fenugreek, to name just a handful of the various spices.

ZAYTOUN

The olive harvest is taken very seriously in Lebanon. The majority of Lebanese dishes are B'zeit, "with oil", and we are of course referring to olive oil. Used to grill and fry dishes, sprinkled on vegetables, grains and salads, and as a dip with *Za'atar* or on its own, olive oil is the IT-girl of the country. Known as *Zaytoun* for "olive" or *Sheik el sofra* for "VIP of the table", everyone in Lebanon will tell you that the best olives come from their village. Olives are harvested in September and October, so if you plan on trying them all out to give your own verdict, we recommend you visit the country in autumn – and make sure to check out Bcheale, known to have the world's oldest olive trees.

Olive oil is preserved in glass jars or in square-shaped steel containers away from light and stored in a cool dry place. It is crucial for Lebanese families to have secured their share of olive oil for the family's yearly consumption. As the main source of fat in most dishes, olive oil enables the Lebanese cuisine to be healthy and low in cholesterol.

Just as the Lebanese don't "Mouneh" alone, you can be bloody sure they don't eat alone either. This warm and welcoming population is known for its endless hospitality towards visitors, even if unexpected (which funnily enough seems to happen quite often). Food

INTRODUCTION

brings families, friends and strangers together. Sharing that food is as meaningful outside the home as it is inside. If you order your own dish at a Lebanese restaurant, the waiter will most definitely look at you funny. Dishes are meant to be put in the middle for all to indulge as a united team-effort. Street vendors, shopkeepers, cafés and restaurants all take this very seriously.

So be prepared to munch down many yummies with some locals, and of course share some happy drinks – cheers!

DRINKS

Lebanon's national drink, *Arak*, is an aniseed-flavoured liquor, also known as "the Milk of Lions" - which sounds somewhat, zoophyliac to us. The spirit (40% - 63%) is a clear, colourless, unsweetened aniseed-flavoured distilled alcoholic drink. The word *Arak* actually means "sweat" in Arabic, go figure. It is served by mixing 1/3 *Arak* with 2/3 water and ice (or 50/50, depending on how strong you like it) giving it a white colour (hence the milk nickname). Other local drinks include beer, Almaza, 961 Beer and Lebanese Brew, AND a delicious selection of Lebanese wines.

Among the oldest wine producing regions in the world, Lebanon has quite a few succulent elixirs to offer, and that number is luckily on the rise. The country has an annual production of about 600,000 cases and the number of wineries went from 5 in 1998 to over 30 in 2014. Lebanese winemakers have favoured French grapes, particularly Cabernet Sauvignon, Merlot and Rhone varieties such as Cinsaut, Carignan and Grenache. The country also has a rich heritage of domestic grapes, which is getting more and more attention. Chateau Musar, Domaine Wardy, and the Obeideh or Merwah grapes make some excellent stuff. To save you time, and liver damage, we've selected a few of our favourite hangout spots to admire, sniff, gargle and mostly gulp down some of that happy juice (see outside Beirut p.169). For those who do not drink booze or are on some weird Gwyneth Paltrow type detox, Lebanon also offers a wide range of non-alcoholic beverages (don't forget that you are in a mostly Muslim country!). On the drinks menu, you will find lemonade, fresh fruit juices, *Jellab* (a soft drink made from raisins and served with pine nuts) or *Ayran* (a stirred yoghurt drink).

MEZZE

Mezze in Lebanon is a true "art de vivre", a real dining experience, and needless to say, should be done properly. When someone asks you if you want Mezze, it actually means "taste" or "snack". The country claims to be the birthplace of appetizers: the practice of serving small dishes began in the 1920s when two small cafés started giving away seeds, nuts, olives and cheese with drinks. These nibbles come in particularly handy when soaking up a couple of glasses of *Arak*.

The whole Mezze experience is incredibly convivial and relaxed, but can sometimes be quite tricky. Some say you should eat the salads first, then the cooked vegetables with the *Sambusac* (pastries) and finally the meat dishes; but most say that there are no rules, and suggest digging in however one feels like. BUT DON'T RUSH! Trust us on this one, Lebanon will never run out of Mezze. These appetizers will stay on the table throughout the whole meal, along with flatbread, which is not just food, but a utensil of its own.

Just tear it and scoop or dip into ANYTHING! You just created an edible spoon.

BREAD

Arabic bread has endlessly varied names, shapes and tastes: *Kmaj*, *Markouk*, *Tlami*, *Saj*. Some are thick (*Tlami*), others, paper thin (*Saj*); some are cooked over a metal dome (which, by lack of imagination, is also called a Saj) or over an openfire (*Hattab*), and others are baked in ovens (*Furn*). All of these variations use water, flour and olive oil. The most important ingredient that goes into all these recipes is technique. Witnessing bakers make bread is quite an experience. They stretch the dough, toss and twirl it round and round, to finally throw it onto the *Saj* and get cooking.

In the Middle East, women used to head down to their village bakery, called the Furn, in order to bake their breads and pastries, while catching up on daily gossip.

Bread is part of every meal and is a staple food in Lebanon. It is so crucial to the Lebanese diet that some Arabic dialects refer to it as "esh", meaning "life."

MAINS

Seconds are as essential as Mezze. You'll be asked at least three times whether you'd like some more, and even if you refuse, expect another serving to miraculously slip onto your plate, so just accept it! The Lebanese are generous and genuinely want to satisfy everyone. By insisting you eat more, even when you are full to bursting, they only mean well.

Dishes are naturally healthy with small amounts of meat and lots of fresh vegetables, grains, herbs and flavour. The most commonly eaten meats are poultry, goat meat in the mountain region and lamb or fish on the coast. Other healthy mains include stuffed courgettes and vine leaves, both very much #occupiedbygarlic, and seasoned with olive oil, herbs and lemon juice. The latter are typical flavours in Lebanon, which are a good nutritious change from heavy gravy sauces, so no need to panic about the amount of food that you'll be gobbling!

At the heart of this wholesome cuisine, are lentils, chickpeas, beans, rice and wheat, making it the ideal destination for vegetarians. These ingredients are cheaper than meat and provide the needed nutrients in a diet that is low in animal proteins. While eating less meat, you will need complementary proteins, which are complete proteins formed by the combination of two non-meat food, such as vegetables with grains, or grains with nuts or seeds. *Hummus bi Tahini*, for example, is a great combination of a grain and seed. You've got chickpeas in the *Hummus* and sesame seeds in the *Tahini*, (a paste of sesame seeds, mashed garlic and lemon juice). *Mjaddara* is an exemplary main in this field: lentils with rice in a one-pot dish. But THE mega protein recipe would be the national dish, *Kibbeh*, which consists of ground lamb combined with cracked wheat paste.

DESSERTS

When it comes to the sweet stuff, the Lebanese sure know how to add sugar to sugar. Not to worry though, as there is always the lighter option of gobbling down a ridiculous amount of fruit. If you want to go local, aim for apples, apricots, oranges, dates, tangerines, persimmons, pomegranates, grapes, melons and of course figs.

Lebanese sweets include pastries such as Baklawa, passed down from the Ottoman Turks. This assortment of flaky pastries is somehow commonly associated with Greek cuisine. The Lebanese, however, prepare it with pistachio nuts drizzled in rose water syrup and the Greeks use walnuts and honey, so it's kind of a "same same but different" type of situation.

Let's be honest here. Lebanon has a long list of desserts and pastries made of almonds, pistachios, sesame seeds, pine nuts or walnuts (apologies to those allergic to nuts), syrup and honey. No need to describe them all here as our index explains what *Awamat, Barazek, Halawa, Maakroun, Maamoul, Namoura* and *Sfouf* are. If you are not a massive fan of cakes, you can also get *Mouhalabieh* (the famous French flan) or *Riz bl Halleb* (rice pudding). The Lebanese are also big on ice cream. You can get any flavour you want, but if you'd like to try something authentic to the region, we recommend the traditional *Bouza bi Halleb* (a milk ice cream with pistachios sprinkled on top).

COFFEE

Black coffee, commonly known as *Al qahwah*, is a nice thing to have after a full meal (so basically every time you eat here).
The strongest option would be the Turkish coffee, which also happens to be the most unattractive option since you might end up with "residue of coffee powder between your teeth". The process consists of roasting and then finely grinding coffee beans that are then boiled in a pot and brewed without adding any sugar. Cardamom is often added, but no cream or milk. Sorry. If you don't feel obliged to prove your manhood to the Lebanese men around you, ask for a Ahweh bayda, the Lebanese white coffee. The caffeine-free drink is made from water, orange blossom water, and sweetened with sugar, if in need of a sugar rush. So, unlike the name suggests, nothing to do with coffee. It is traditionally thought to facilitate digestion and soothe the nerves. Or you can just ask for tea.

And then it's nap time.

RELIGIOUS CUSTOMS

Most Lebanese people are Muslims, and belong to one of the three different factions: Sunni, Shiite, or Druze. Lebanon is also home to a large Christian population and almost one-quarter of its citizens are members of the Maronite Church, a division of the Roman Catholic Church. Other Christians in Lebanon include followers of Greek Orthodoxy, Roman Catholicism, and Protestantism. Lebanon is the only Arab country in the world with such a diversity of Muslims and Christians. Despite bitter disagreements between the different groups, the people of both religions continue to enjoy their own traditional festive celebrations, which of course include lots and lots of food.

Muslims celebrate several holidays throughout the year, though probably none are as important as the holiday of Ramadan. During the entire ninth month of the Islamic calendar, Muslims fast between sunrise and sunset. So imagine for a moment that for 30 days every year - from sunrise to sunset each day - you were not allowed to eat any food or drink any liquids, including water to rinse your mouth from toothpaste or your must-have caffeine shot. For Muslims, the month of Ramadan serves as a time of self-reflection, gratitude and atonement. The religious concept of fasting in Islam is to show the value of the many things that are often overlooked in life. The act of fasting helps to truly appreciate the great bounties (food, water, etc.) that people usually take for granted.

The day usually begins when Muslims wake up before dawn to eat a pre-dawn breakfast

Mohammed Al-Amin Mosque in Downtown (p.75)

meal (known as Suhoor in Arabic) with their families. In some villages, a man beats a drum through the streets, attempting to wake people up before the sun rises so that they may enjoy an early breakfast and not die of starvation during the day. A typical pre-dawn breakfast might include grapefruit, flatbread with olive oil, a boiled egg, a cup of Laban (yogurt), and tea. Then begins the count-down before sunset when food can once again be eaten in evening meals known as Iftaar. Muslims generally break their fast by eating dates, to emulate the Prophet Muhammad, who broke his fast the same way.

Dates are apparently easy to digest, decrease hunger and prepare the stomach after fasting. They are rich in sugary energy and adjust the acidity of blood. So no wonder this tradition has been around for a while! A typical Iftaar menu begins with juice, such as Amar el Din (apricot nectar), dried fruits (hence the dates) and a traditional lentil soup, followed by a variety of cold and hot Mezze (obv!). The main course varies every day: among those offered are the fish-based Sayadiyeh and Moloukhieh, a thick vegetable stew served with rice and garnish. Fresh fruit, desserts and hot tea or coffee brings the feast to an end. To witness the magic of Iftaar, have an after-sunset dinner in West Beirut (don't go there for lunch during Ramadan, that would just be inconsiderate).

Eid al-Fitr, also known as "festival that breaks the fast", or "Sweet Eid", marks the end of Ramadan when millions of Muslim boys and girls get super excited. Mostly because of the sugar rush from the sweet dishes served on this occasion and, of course, because of the gifts. It's not exactly comparable to Christmas or Hanukkah, as the lesson to be learned from the Muslim holy month of Ramadan and Eid is actually about the spirit of gratitude.

The "Feast of the Sacrifice", Eid al-Adha, or "Salty Eid" (mainly because of all the savouries) is the second biggest religious holiday. It lasts for three or fours days, but the dates vary, drifting approximately 11 days earlier each year in the Gregorian calendar. Muslims who can afford to, sacrifice their best halal[1] domestic animals (usually a cow, but can also be a goat or a sheep depending on the region) as a symbol of Abraham's willingness to sacrifice his only son. The sacrificed animals have to have reached a certain age and met certain quality standards or else they are considered unacceptable sacrifices. The meat is then divided into three parts. The family retains one third; another third is given to relatives, friends and neighbours; and the remaining third is given to the poor and needy, (though the division is purely optional). A huge barbecue with loads of *Kebab*s (boneless meat that has been meshed and fried or roasted) is tradition on the first day. And we're sure that you'll be happy to know that the animal's fried liver is served at breakfast (yum yum yum).

Lebanon is the only Middle Eastern nation where Christmas is an official holiday. It has many specific customs, mostly comparable to French traditions (because of French colonialism), though some are distinct and unique to this country. For Lebanese Christians, Christmas is an occasion to renew friendships and for reconciliation. Also celebrated by Lebanese Muslims, families in Lebanon embrace Christmas by decorating their houses with Christmas trees, while all major roads and streets are decorated with Christmas lights and "Crèches" (French for Nativity crib). Villages in Lebanon make large bonfires where everyone gathers around to tell stories and sing songs. On Saint Barbara's Day, which falls a couple of weeks before Christmas, the Lebanese plant seeds, like chickpeas, wheat grains, beans and lentils in cotton wool, and

---

1. Is any object or action which is permissable to use or engage in, according to Islamic Law.

water them every day. By Christmas time, the seeds have sprouted, and the Lebanese use them to bring something different to their "Crèche". Homes are decorated with tinsel, and Christmas trees are often adorned with orange peels cut into various shapes.

On Christmas Eve, the conventional dinner includes turkey, roasted duck or chicken, with *Tabouleh*, rice and *Kibbeh*. Pastries such as honey cake and the traditional French Christmas cake "Bûche De Noel" (a chocolate ice cream cake) are next on the menu. When Lebanese Christians attend midnight mass, "Papa Noël" (or some other dude who didn't want to go to church) puts the gifts under the tree.

Christmas lunch is considered the most important meal of the season. The whole family gathers at the home of the eldest male member, be it the grandfather or the eldest son, and enjoys a meal similar to the one above. Visiting friends and family at Christmas has become tradition. Prior to a large chicken or turkey lunch, most guests are offered liqueur, coffee and sugar-coated almonds to snack on. *Meghli*, a sweet, cinnamon pudding, which is made to celebrate the birth of a child, is also made for Christmas to celebrate the birth of Jesus.

All Lebanese people exchange gifts on December 25th except for the Christian Armenian Lebanese who do it on the Epiphany on January 6th, which is also an official holiday in Lebanon. This is again very much influenced by the French. The famous "Galette des rois" (which translates as King's Cake) is filled with almond paste and hides a little figurine inside. Tradition has it that whoever gets the charm – without choking on it – becomes king for the day.

Holiday season is a prefect time to go skiing. And guess what. You can ski in Lebanon. And yes, you can also eat fondue.

Easter is also a big deal in this country. A little birdie told us that Lebanon was ranked #3 in celebrating Easter (after Argentina and Greece, but honestly we don't get how the ranking system works). For Lent, which lasts 40 days until Good Friday, people fast and adopt a strict vegan-diet. Lent is broken on Easter Sunday with an absolute feast of lamb and lots of egg breaking. The Easter egg game is called "Biis-Biis", and consists of kids competing to see who has the strongest, most unbreakable hard-boiled egg. Of course there is chocolate for dessert, but the more traditional choice would be *Maamoul* (date or nut-filled teacakes). A melt-in-your-mouth experience.

As in any other country, history and politics are another good excuse to eat, feed, dine and munch. So please, pig away on Labour Day (May 1st) and Independence Day (November 22nd).

As you've probably realised by now, the Lebanese are not just serious about their *Hummus*; they are serious about food...period.

SHORTLISTS

OUR WINNERS
Tawlet (p.143), Em Sherif (p.106), Abou Hassan (p.66), Al Mayass (p.93)

OUR FAVOURITE HU-MOOSE IN TOWN
Hummus Awarma at Fadel (p.191), Hummus at Varouj (p.154), Hummus with pine nuts at Abou Hassan (p.66)

OUR FAVOURITE FISH RESTAURANTS
Al Sultan Ibrahim (p.76 & p.180), Chez Sami (p.181), Le Phenicien (p.162 & p.210)

OUR FAVOURITE FOR BOOZY DINNERS
Epicery (p.137), Happy Prince (p.138), Momo's (p.81)

OUR FAVOURITE CURES FOR HANGOVERS
Frosty Palace (p.137), Margherita (p.125), Jaï (p.50)

Tawlet has some of Beirut's most delicious cuisine. See p.143 for more details

A WEEKEND IN BEIRUT WITH YOUR LOVER

- **A** Julep's
- **B** La plage
- **C** Dragonfly
- **D** Anise
- **E** Albergo rooftop
- **F** Souk el Tayeb
- **G** Kayan
- **H** Al Mayass
- **I** Sydney
- **J** Casablanca

A WEEKEND IN BEIRUT WITH YOUR LOVER, *GRRRR!*

FRIDAY

You've just landed, it's past 6pm, therefore clearly time to go get yourself a well deserved drink – or two – at **Julep's** (p.82). Once you've felt that buzz, head over to **La Plage** (p.70) for a romantic dinner by the sea. After your meal, if you can keep your hands off of each other, get one last drink at **Dragonfly** (p.128) or **Anise** (p.147), which are two cosy bars that serve some jazzy cocktails.

SATURDAY

You might be a baller and be staying at the Albergo hotel, in which case check out **the Albergo rooftop** (p.91) for a sumptuous breakfast (FYI: they also allow in non-ballers). From there, walk towards Downtown and wander around until you reach the city's famous farmer's market **Souk El Tayeb** (p.75). Have a look or a bite. To digest, why not go for a long walk and prepare yourselves for a not-so-light dinner. Before sitting down to eat, get an aperitif at **Kayan** (p.129), but try not to snack on their nibbles! Dinner at our favourite Armenian restaurant **Al Mayass** (p.93) is truly worth keeping your stomach empty for. If the heavy food hasn't made you too sleepy, then **Sydney's** (p.69) is your best option for a private late night drink.

The Albergo's rooftop is one of Beirut's most romantic spots (p.91)

SUNDAY

Take your time and lounge in bed (you're on holiday, merde!) –and once that's done, get your ass to **Casablanca** (p.66) for a tasty romantic brunch.

A WEEKEND IN BEIRUT WITH YOUR FRIENDS

- **A** Varouj
- **B** Internazionale
- **C** Torino
- **D** Al Falamanki
- **E** Tawlet
- **F** Vyvyan's
- **G** Epicery
- **H** Em Sherif
- **I** Momo's
- **J** Abou Hassan

A WEEKEND IN BEIRUT WITH YOUR FRIENDS

(take photos! you might not remember much….)

FRIDAY

You just made it through customs (phew) and are starting to feel a little peckish. Quickly drop off your luggage and get in a taxi, destination → **Varouj** (p.154). The not-so-welcoming Armenian owner will probably tell you to fuck off but hang in tight. No menu, no questions asked but some amazing food in good company (at least, we hope so for your sake). Dinner's been gulped? Time for drinks! **Internazionale** (p.149) is where to get the party started and **Torino** (p.129) is where you should end it. Craving a little midnight (or 4am) snack? **Al Falamanki** (p.104) is open 24/7 and ideal for big friendly groups.

SATURDAY

Feeling like death, round 2? **Tawlet's** (p.143) healthy and delicious cuisine will give you a much-needed boost.

If you're walking down Mar Mikhael, then why not get a quick drink (you know you want to ... it's the best antidote!) at **Vyvyan's** (p.149) or at **Epicery** (p.137) and ask Sako the bartender to make you the one with the cucumber. He'll know. Dinner has to be at **Em Sherif** (p.106). This place might look a bit bling bling at first, but is truly an outstanding culinary experience that shouldn't be missed. Next stop: **Momo's** (p.81) for some drinks and groovy dancing.

SUNDAY

Yep, we know how you feel. "Never again"? Sure... In the meantime, a recent study showed that vitamin B6 helps to cure hangovers and guess where you can find some of that? In chickpeas! That's right: get some Hummus (with pine nuts) at **Abou Hassan** (p.66). Try to spot these two guys (right and bottom) to get that necessary caf- feine shot with a nice **Tahinov Hats** (p.158) for dessert.

A Tahinov hats vendor in Bourj Hammoud

A WEEKEND IN BEIRUT ON A TIGHT ASS BUDGET

- **A** Baromètre
- **B** Café de Prague
- **C** Dany's
- **D** February 30
- **E** Furn Michel Saade
- **F** Mikhael
- **G** Mikhael
- **H** Em Nazih & Coop d'État
- **I** Torino
- **J** Zataar w Zeit
- **K** Apo Kebab
- **L** Basterma Mano

(F) M. Sahyoun & Sahyoun Falafel

A WEEKEND IN BEIRUT ON A TIGHT ASS BUDGET

FRIDAY

Beirut might not be as cheap as you thought, but at least the city's most affordable places sure aren't boring. It's Friday night, let's not waste any time and dive right into it. Start your evening off at **Barometre** (p.50) by dancing to some Arab tunes while stuffing yourself with Mezze. Continue the celebrations anywhere in Hamra for some cheap swills (including Café De Prague or Dany's); or if you feel like a good cocktail and are prepared to splurge a little (alcohol may have that effect on you, but control yourself!) head down to **February 30** (p.55) Happy Friday!

SATURDAY

Drink some water, perhaps take a shower and then get yourself a *Manouche* (or three) at **Furn Michel Saade** (p.99). This tasty breakfast will help you forget all the embarrassing things you might've said, or worse, done last night! Still hungry? (Hangovers can be a bitch, we know). If so, walk to **M. Sahyoun and Sahyoun Falafel** (p.113) for some luscious *Falafels*. These two shops belong to the Sahyoun brothers, who are competing for … well we're not too sure, but try them both and let us know which one you dig best. Once that's done, get some sweet stuff at **Mikhael** (p.102). Stroll about, mingle and … uuuuuummm … what's that you said, ready for dinner?

Walk (although the richer locals might disapprove and give you a dirty look from their BMW) down to Gemmayzeh and get to **Em Nazih** (p.120). For cheap drinks just climb the stairs (no lift, sorry) to the rooftop bar **Coop D'Etat** (p.120) and when they kick your drunk-ass out, zigzag your way to **Torino** (p.129). Once the munchies have started to kick in, turn right next door to **Zaatar w Zeit** (p.131) for some snacks.

SUNDAY

Blend in with the Armenians at Bourj Hammoud and grab one of the yummiest *Kebabs* you'll ever chomp at **Apo** (p.157), or try some local cured meat at **Basterma Mano** (p.158). Now go right back to bed and doze off 'til Monday, you filthy bastard. And if you're really broke, then you can always go here (↓).

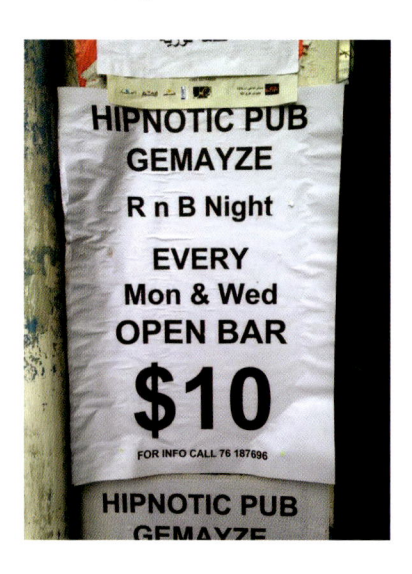

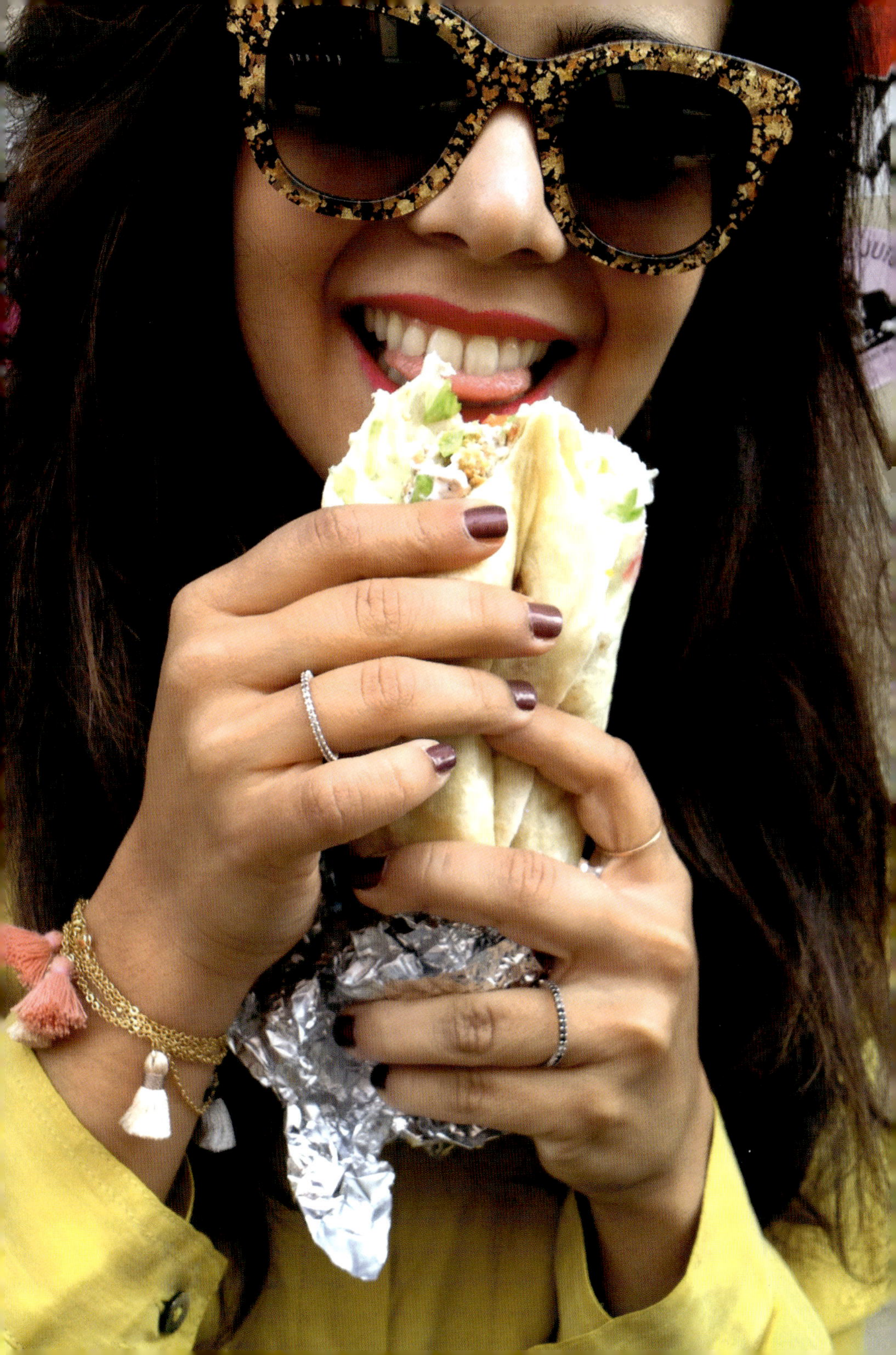

REVIEWS LEGEND

◐ = Recommended for breakfast or Brunch

☀ = Has a terrace or rooftop

REVIEWS

Our guide isn't simply about food, it's about good food. Unlike others, we won't recommend the cool, the hip, the beautiful and the charming. Our goal is to lead you to places that ooze taste and flavour. This may include the ugly, but will save you from ever having to encounter the bad.

What better way to end an out-of-this-world meal, than with some good funky cocktails? Our guide only recommends the best cocktail bars in town, so if your aim is to get cheap drinks at a fun bar that will get you buzzed ASAP, please drop us an email (we@dont-believeinjetlag.com) as we've got quite a few addresses to share, as well as memories – or lack thereof.

Giving exact information on location, opening hours or telephone numbers is close to impossible in this country. Even though we've honestly tried our best, we still recommend you check web or Facebook pages for precise details and changes of address. Small family businesses are the most difficult ones when it comes to determining opening hours. We cannot guarantee that the father won't get tired and close the doors a few hours earlier, or that the son won't accidentally click snooze, fall back asleep and forget to open the family shop. We apologize if these situations happen, and recommend you take them with a pinch of salt and a smile, as this is Lebanon!

HAMRA & CLEMENCEAU

A Earth Market
B Gustav
C Nutellissimo
D Amal Bohsali
E Aunty Salwa
F Bread Republic
G Bagatelle
H Barometre
I Jaï
J Dar Bistro & Books 
K Kabab-Ji
L Socrate
M T-Marbouta
N February 30
O Garcia's
P Abou Afif
Q Barbar
R Orfali
S Marrouche
T Zaatar w Zeit

HAMRA & CLEMENCEAU

A ctive Hamra is a commercial area filled with eateries, cafes, bars, cars and pedestrians. The neighbourhood is where you'll find many expats living the life, students from the American University of Beirut pigging out on Bliss Street and strollers walking about. Traffic can get pretty crazy, but the cheap bars and restaurants make up for the ride. Linking Hamra to Downtown is Clemenceau. This residential area used to be one of the city's most cosmopolitan neighbourhoods prior to the war. Nowadays it permits a sweet and calm escape from chaotic adjacent Hamra.

MARKETS

A EARTH MARKET
Alley connecting Hamra St with Makdissi St, next to Radio Shack
Tuesday from 9am-2pm

This quaint little market tucked away on a tiny alleyway in Hamra, features 15 small-scale farmers and producers from different villages around Lebanon, who cook and sell their local jams, cedar honey, Arabic bread, *Mouwaraka* (a thinly rolled pastry filled with walnuts, almonds and honey), *Kishk*, *Za'atar* and other spices. We recommend you grab lunch at **Bread Republic** (see p.47) at their outdoor tables as it's only a few steps away.

#farmersmarket #tasteeverything

Earth Market

SHOPS

B GUSTAV
Antoine Gemayel St. Hamra
Telephone: +961 (0)1 747199
Monday–Saturday from 7am-12am;Sunday from noon-12am

The two brothers behind Gustav clearly had no idea what impact they'd have on everyone's love handles. From red velvet cakes (LBP 6.500/4.5$), cardamom blueberry macaroons (LBP 2.000/1.5$), to crème brulée (LBP 6.000/4$), their mouth-watering indulgences have got all of Hamra coming for more.

#sweetinnovations #pomegranitetart #vanillafromtahiti

C NUTELISSIMO
Hamra Main St. Hamra
Telephone: +961 (0)3 468936
Daily from 10am-noon

Who loves Orange Soda Nutella? Everyone. This tiny boutique tucked away in frantic Hamra sells Nutella based everything. From cupcakes, brownies, crepes, to muffins, you are absolutely sure to get some extra junk in your trunk here.

#sweettooth #monthlycravings

Ⓓ AMAL BOHSALI

Alfred Nobel St. Hamra
Telephone: +961 (0)1 354400
Daily from 9am-8pm

Authentic Arabic delights, top-notch quality – from Knefe, Baklawa, to Maamoul, this sweet shop has it all. If you're feeling cheeky, try the 1kg package of assorted pastries (LBP 82.000/54$) to get a bit(e) of everything.

#moresweetstuff #sugaroverdose

RESTAURANTS

E AUNTY SALWA
Baalbaki Bldg, Hamra
Telephone: +961 (0)1 749746
Monday-Saturday from 8am-5pm

As enjoyable (and fattening) as Lebanese food can be, it remains heavy, greasy and not always the healthiest; we've sadly acquired the spots and cellulite to prove it. At Aunty Salwa the food is never fried and is devoid of slimy oil. The canteen is mostly vegetarian, but the dish of the day may surprise you and be a meaty treat. The hostess greets guests with her Colgate smile and bids farewell with a pleasant bill. Meal for two LBP 35.000/23.5$.

#healthyhomecooking

F BREAD REPUBLIC
Nehme Yafet St. Hamra
Telephone: +961 (0)1 739040
Daily from 7.30am-11pm

Great for people watching and expat spotting in Hamra, or to chill and take a breather in Achrafieh, Bread Republic is a healthy breakfast and lunch spot. Serving organic vegetables and local produce, dishes are tastefully wholesome. Egg worshippers: order the *Tabouleh* omelette (LBP 11.500/7.5$) for the perfect west-meets-orient type of dish. For lunch, we recommend the melted brie on walnut bread or the spaghettinis with spicy octopus. For desert, hop into their Hamra bakery and try any of their amazing pastries.

Food at Bread Republic is always served fresh

Recommended drink: dark lemonade, mixed with blackcurrant and blackberry.

#organiclunchspot #slowfood #goodspottogosolo

Bagatelle's chorizo in red wine cocotte

BAGATELLE
Jeanne d'Arc St. Hamra
Telephone: +961 (0) 1 342842
Monday–Sunday from 9am-12am

If you happen to be seeking a groovy French bistro, with an Italian twist, then look no further! With its adorable little front terrace, this Amélie Poulain type of bar à vin is the perfect place to savour some funky food while listening to jazz. Beirut is not the most adventurous of places - when it comes to food at least - so by funky food, we mean some traditional dishes with an edge. Their use of organic vegetables creates beautiful flavours and, from truffle chicken to calamari risotto, the aromas are rich. Their pizzas are super duper thin. We especially relished their goat cheese, mozzarella, fresh cream, pear slices, prosciutto and rocket leaves pizza (LBP 24.000/16$).

Recommended dish: chorizo in red wine cocotte (LBP 16.500/11$).
#winelovers #gettingtipsyatlunch

H BAROMETRE
Blue Building, Makhoul St. Hamra
Telephone: +961 (0)3 678998
Daily from 7pm-1.30am

Oriental dancing, loud music and tasty homemade Mezze at a bargain (LBP 5.000-7.000/3-5$) is what boho Barometre is all about. While packed with everyone from intellectuals to women baring their cleavage, this special place doesn't see many tourists – so follow their lead.
#bringearplugs

I JAÏ
Mexico St. Clemenceau
Telephone Restaurant: +961 (0)1 745940;
Delivery: +961 (0)1 341940
Monday-Saturday from 11am-11pm

The Lebanese aren't big fans of waiting, so with its one table and open view on all the action, Jaï is more frequently used for its impeccable delivery services. The Thai-meets-Indian eatery offers selections for the skinnies, like the glass noodle salad (crunchy, with very few noodles but filled with taste) and for the gourmands, like the very rich Nasi Goreng or Korma Curry. Only downside: no desserts.

Recommended dish: general tsao chicken (smokey sauce chicken with jasmine rice) LBP 19.000/12$.

#hangovers #skinnybitches #fatties #healthfreaks #anyone

A convivial meal at Jaï's only table

J DAR (BISTRO AND BOOKS)
Rome St. Hamra
Telephone: +961 (0)1 373348
Daily from 8am-12am

In ancient Arabic, Dar means the sitting room of a house, which is rather fitting here. Tucked away behind a cute garden-esque terrace, this bookstore-meets-café is the ideal place to get lost for breakfast, smoothies and lunch. The tasty dishes are a crisscross between international and Oriental cuisine. It's oddly not very known among the Lebanese, and we believe this may be deliberate as most come here to escape, therefore keep it a secret.

Recommended drink: cinnamon iced tea.

#detoxfood #bookworm

Saucy couscous at Dar

K KABAB-JI

Hamra St. Hamra and Bliss St. Hamra
Telephone: +961 (0)1 741555
Daily from 8am-12am

As the name suggests, *Kebabs* are involved. This healthy chain has been making banging fast food since 1993.

Recommended *Kebab*: Khachkhach (Ground meat, kneaded with house-blend spices and parsley. Sandwich with *Hummus* & pickled cucumber) LBP 5.000/3.5$. Recommended smaller dish: *Lahm Ba'ajine Halabi* (Crusty home-made dough topped with seasoned meat and mixed with pomegranate syrup and spices) LBP 3.500/2.5$.

#cheekykebabonthego

L SOCRATE

Sidani St. Hamra
Hotline 1530
Daily from 9am-11pm

Socrate is a wisely traditional caterer and restaurant. The menu consists of home-cooked meals with 5 dishes of the day and plenty of fixed delicacies. Many years ago, this eatery used to be the canteen of AUB (the American University of Beirut). Judging by its older crowd, it's now the canteen of its alumni.

Recommended dish: *Kibbeh labanieh* (in garlic and herbs yogurt sauce over rice - LBP 16.000/10$).

#homeychilledoutmeal

THE FOOD GUIDE: BEIRUT ON A PLATE

Lamb Biryani with cashews at Socrate

T-MARBOUTA

Hamra Square Center, Hamra St. Hamra
Telephone: +961 (0)1 350274
Daily from 10am-1am (Open until 2am on Fridays and Saturdays)

Tucked away in a shopping centre on Hamra's main street, this quaint café serves tasty platters and Mezze to share. This humble hangout is filled with freelancers typing away and literati chatting all day. What really caught our attention (and palette) though, was their Aubergine *Musaqa* (LBP 7.000/4.6$).

#sweetandsimple

BARS

FEBRUARY 30
The Alleyway, Jeanne D'Arc St. Hamra
Telephone: +961 7 6994405
Opening hours Daily 10am-3.30am

A suitably unreal label for a place that often gives us blackouts, February 30 does exist though, in a country where the weather remains warm and people sit outside. Flowing juicy cocktails (LBP 15.000/10$) will get you boozed up in no time, and with its Alice in Wonderland-like décor where seats are glued to the ceiling, you soon won't be sure whether the place is a trip, or if you're the one trippin'.

#checkouttheirnapkins

GARCIA'S
Makdessi St. Hamra
Telephone: +961 (0)1 738538
Daily from 6pm-3am

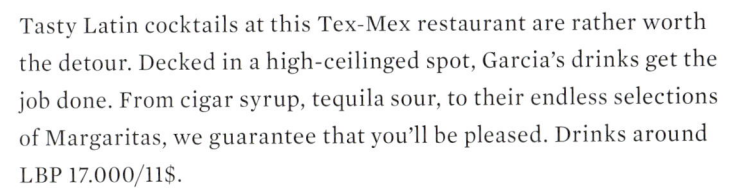

Tasty Latin cocktails at this Tex-Mex restaurant are rather worth the detour. Decked in a high-ceilinged spot, Garcia's drinks get the job done. From cigar syrup, tequila sour, to their endless selections of Margaritas, we guarantee that you'll be pleased. Drinks around LBP 17.000/11$.

#biggroups

STREET FOOD

ⓟ ABOU AFIF
Sidani St. Hamra
Telephone: +961 (0)3 235444
Daily from 11am-7pm

Located right by Marrouche (see p.57), Abou Afif prepares tasty sandwiches right before your eyes. Watch the owner's funky hand gestures as he crafts your snack and hands it to you – he's clearly no beginner.

ⓠ BARBAR
Omar Bin Abdul Aziz St. Hamra
Telephone: +96 (0)1 753330
Open 24/7

Having first opened in 1982 as a small bakery, Barbar has come a long way since. The 24/7 joint offers the best junk food for late night cravings. At any hour of the day, you'll find crowds munching on some of its delicious Falafels, Manouche, *Kebab*s, pastries, *Shawarma*, fresh juices, ice cream: you name it. If you're about to pass out, or just woke up and feel like shit, pick up the phone coz they deliver.

Recommended dish: the Francisco (cheese and chicken sandwich with mayo and soy sauce).

🐦 #feelinglikeapig #cheapandgreasystuff #amen

R ORFALI
Mahatma Ghandi St. Hamra
Telephone: +96 (0)1 747787
Daily from 10am-12am Delivery available

See review in Achrafieh & Monnot & Sodeco p.112

S MARROUCHE
Sidani St. Hamra
Telephone: +961 (0)1 743188
Open 24/7

Preparing great *Shawarmas* and *Falafels* since 1920, Marrouche is rumored to be the basis of London's "Marroush" chain. The menu's in Arabic, so we recommend you try your luck, point away, and hope for the best! OR, if you're not the spontaneous and adventurous type, attempt to order in English or check out our index (see p.216).

#hangovercure #munchies #24hours

T ZAATAR W ZEIT
Bliss St. Hamra
Telephone: +961 (0)1 544338
Open 24/7

See review in Gemmayzeh & Saifi p.131

BLISS STREET
Hamra
Open 24/7

Facing the American University of Beirut, this Disneyland for hangovers is packed with fast food vendors. Burgers, Manouche, hot dogs, ice creams and juices are all yours within a 5-minute reach. We especially recommend Bliss House, which has become an institution in Lebanon. If you'd like to remain local, try their delicious chicken *Shawarma* with garlic paste, which includes a sexy stinky breath for the rest of your day! If you're getting slightly fed up of Arabic food, (it happens), their Philly steak sandwich isn't bad either.

#foodisbliss

Moist Lamb at Bliss House

• MAR ELIAS •

A Al Rifai

B Le Professeur

MAR ELIAS

This popular shopping district is known for its array of shoes and clothes, as well as its never-ending traffic. Most of its boutiques are local and cheap, making it the ideal place to hunt for bargains.

SHOPS

A AL RIFAI

Al Rifai Bldg, Corniche Mazraa
Telephone: +961 (0)1 705105
Daily from 7am-10pm

Now selling in numerous shops, including the airport and abroad, Al Rifai has invaded the country and become Lebanon's key nut-vendor. Their pistachios and other nuts, whether spiced, flavoured or kept natural are all of a top-notch quality.

#nutsfornuts

RESTAURANTS

🅱 LE PROFESSEUR

Mar Elias St. Mazraa
Telephone: +961 (0)1 703666
Daily from 8am-2pm

Le professeur presents a rather extensive Lebanese menu filled with Mezze, which attracts quite a crowd. We have to admit that this place chose quite a fitting name as, if they offered any, we'd be the first to take part in their cooking lessons. (LBP 12.000/8$ for 5 dishes)

#casuallunch #suitableforvegetarians

Mezze in Beirut are always served fresh

RAOUCHÉ & AIN EL MREISSEH & ZAITUNAY BAY

- **A** Abou Hassan
- **B** Casablanca
- **C** Four Seasons Hotel
- **D** La Petite Maison
- **E** St Elmo's
- **F** Sydney's Club
- **G** La plage
- **H** Deck Café
- **I** Feluka
- **J** Le pêcheur
- **K** Karam al Bahr

RAOUCHÉ & AIN EL MREISSEH & ZAITUNAY BAY

—

Welcome to the city's coastline: from the street-vendors and joggers on the authentic Corniche, to the cafés and shops on luxurious Miami-esque Zaitunay Bay, this area is ideal for lovers to admire the sunrise or sunset, while enjoying the area's succulent food. Whether grabbing a bite on the go, checking out a fish restaurant or going high-end, make sure to walk by Raouché's pigeon's rock; you may have seen a photo of the boulder before, as it's become a sort of emblem of Beirut.

RESTAURANTS

🅐 ABOU HASSAN

Salah Eddine Ayoubi St. Karakas, Raouché
Telephone: +961 (0)1 741725
Daily from 9am–12.30am

Enjoyably cheap southern Lebanese cuisine filled with spices and flavours. The frakeh (raw sheep mixed with spices and *Burghul*) and their Mujaddara hamra (red lentils, tomatoes, burnished onions and *Burghul*) are quite something.

🐦 #localspot #bringyourownbooze

🅑 CASABLANCA

Dar Al Mreisseh St. Ain El Mreisseh
Telephone: +961 (0)1 369334
Tuesday-Saturday from 12.30pm-4pm, 7pm-12am;
Sunday from 11am-3pm, 8pm-12am

If you ask anyone in Beirut what their favourite restaurant is, the majority will undoubtedly say Casablanca. Tucked away on a side street, in an old high-ceilinged Lebanese house facing the beautiful seashore, this brasserie offers exquisite fusion cuisine, mixing far eastern flavours with western twists. From the sake martini (beware, it's rather strong!), and the salty and tender grilled octopus, to the mouth-watering fried gyoza filled with shrimp and calamari; everything on the menu is divine. You may munch with a free conscience - as Casablanca is known for only using organic products, most of which come straight from the owner's farm in

Salt & pepper calamari at Casablanca

the countryside. To add a pinch of humour to your meal, the goofy waiters all wear comical cartoon ties and enjoy teasing their regulars. This place is very much "in" socially speaking, and in terms of food – missing out would be a sin. To order: the Cheesecake. Described by many as the best in town - LBP 16.500/10$.

#sundaybrunch #weekenddinner #notsocheap

C FOUR SEASONS HOTEL
Professeur Wafic Sinno Avenue, Minet El Hosn
Telephone: +961 (0)1 761 000
Breakfast every day until noon

If you're a breakfast person, then get your ass here ASAP. The unlimited buffet (LBP 52.000/36$ per person) offers some mind-blowing Danish pastries (including cinnamon cro-nuts!), fruits,

Lebanese pastries, eggs and anything else you never knew you craved. On top of that, the staff are at your beck and call.

#morningglory #skiplunch

D LA PETITE MAISON
Hotel Le Vendome, Rafis Al Hariri St. Ain El Mreisseh
Telephone: +961 (0)1 368300
Daily from 12.30pm-3.30pm; 7pm-11pm

Originally launched in Nice in 1988, La Petite Maison has been popping up around the world ever since. The service is impeccable and the food is exceedingly good, especially the grilled veal chops glazed in their secret sweet paste (LBP 85.000/57$).

#painfulbill #whitetableclothesandsilverware #niçoisecuisine

E ST ELMO'S
Beirut Marina, Zaitunay Bay
Telephone: +961 (0)1 368276
Monday–Saturday from 10am-12am;
Sunday from 10am-11pm

Considering it is located on Zaitunay Bay, where the rent is unimaginably high, we're not too sure how long this place will manage to survive and stay open. The food can be hit-or-miss, orgasmic at times, and very disappointing at others. It's a great spot for brunch though, with their funky variations of Bloody Marys (especially the oyster one! LBP 28.000/18$) and beautiful fried mac and cheese balls (LBP 16.000/10$).

#asailorsheaven #trytheircookies

RAOUCHÉ & AIN EL MREISSEH & ZAITUNAY BAY

Fried Mac & Cheese balls and a Bloody Mary at St Elmo's

🟠 SYDNEY'S CLUB
Hotel Le Vendome, Rafis Al Hariri St. Ain El Mreisseh
Telephone: +961 (0)1 369280
Daily 24hours

Being Beirut's only upscale restaurant open 24/7, there's a fair chance you may encounter some prostitutes if you drop by at 3 AM. This shouldn't stop you from going though (although we secretly hope it entices you instead). With its striking view of the sea, cosy décor and exceptional international food, especially their signature beetroot risotto (LBP 32.000/21$), Sydney's never disappoints. After your meal, why not check out their cigar lounge area for a cheeky puff from one of their 45-brand menu.

🐦 #drunkenindulgences #grownups #businesspeople #whiskey

FISH RESTAURANTS

Lebanese fish restaurants can be outstanding, yet sadly repetitive. From the expected Mezze, to the fresh selection of fish served any way you wish, to the desserts, it's pretty much always the same shebang. What somewhat differentiates them is the setting –if that. Don't get us wrong; they are absolutely worth the detour as the quality of the food is superb. Which one to go to though, is entirely up to you.

La Plage

G LA PLAGE
Rafik Hariri Ave. Ain El Mreisseh
Telephone: +961 (0)1 366222
Daily from noon-1am

Lunch or dine in a beautiful setting down by the pier, among la crème de la crème of Beirut. If it weren't for the obvious, you'd think you were in Saint Tropez. During warm nights, sit down by the pier and gaze into your lover's eyes.

#35dollarsforadipinthepool #uppercrustbeirutis

🅗 THE DECK CAFÉ (SPORTING CLUB)

Chouran St. El-Manara, Raouché
Telephone: +961 (0)1742483
Daily from noon-12am

For a more laid back meal, in a 70's beach setting: come here and order the fried cauliflower with the *Tahini* sauce!

🐦 #stuckinthe70s #decksonthebeach

🅘 FELUKA (SPORTING CLUB)

Chouran St. El-Manara, Raouché
Telephone: +961 (0)1742483
Daily from noon-12am

Deliciously yummy, but oddly always closed for renovation ... try your luck?

🅙 LE PÊCHEUR

Rafik Hariri Ave. Ain El Mreisseh
Telephone: +961 (0)1 374752
Daily from noon-1am

Ideally calm and chilled-out to enjoy your very own little feast.

🐦 #dolladolla

🅚 KARAM AL BAHR

Beirut Marina, Zaitunay Bay
Telephone: +961 (0)1 360777
Daily from noon-12am

Enjoy traditional seafood while watching yachts and pretend you're in Miami. Get the fried calamari for LBP 21.000/14$.

🐦 #seafoodcravings

STREET FOOD

Joggers and strollers are often found on this wide street along the seacoast. This being Lebanon: where there are people, there is food. Vendors selling coffee, freshly squeezed orange juice, catch-of-the-day fish, corn and spicy beans eaten with lime, are doing their thing, i.e. doing whatever it takes to get your attention. We highly recommend the beans, they are pretty delicious.

Oddly enough, one of the tastiest things we've had in Beirut are Syrian roasted almonds covered in sea salt, which can be found on this sea-front as well as around the city.

We wish we could give you an exact location for all of the above, but it's really just a matter of luck.

A street food vendor on
the Corniche

• DOWNTOWN •

A Souk El Tayeb
B Aziz
C Al Sultan Brahim
D Balthus
E BRGR & Co
F Cocteau
G Indigo on the roof
H Kampaï
I Mandaloun sur Mer
J Momo at the Souks
K Iris
L Julep's

DOWNTOWN

Beirut's newly reconstructed Downtown, which had brutally suffered from the war but has been put back into shape, now looks brand new. As the city's central district, Downtown houses Beirut's souks (warning: not a Middle-Eastern bazaar, only new shops here, before you get disappointed), the martyr's square, the great mosque, the city's most upscale restaurants and much more. Although the area can look like a ghost town on quieter days, the sublime architecture and setting make it a wonderful walk on any chosen day.

MARKETS

A SOUK EL TAYEB

Tablos St. Beirut Souks, Downtown
Telephone: +961 (0)1 989041
Saturday from 9am-2pm

As Lebanon's very own open-air farmer's market, taking place every Saturday morning, Souk El Tayeb is a very special place for foodies. Created in 2004, its aim is to preserve the country's food traditions by promoting small farms and helping them compete with industrial agri-businesses. 60 different producers present their products each Saturday, ranging from honey, fruits, olive oil, pastries, marzipan, to homemade crafts.

#organic #dontforgetyourfiveaday #chefssupermarket

SHOPS

B AZIZ

Fakhreddine St. Kantari
Telephone: +961 (0)1 358001
Monday to Saturday from 7.30am-9pm
Sunday from 8am-1pm

Looking for a nice bottle of wine? Feel like some truffled camembert (LBP 40.000/26$ for the small one) or foie gras? Craving charcuterie and organic vegetables? Aziz is your best bet. From festive ready-made stuffed turkeys to anything really, this delicatessen boutique sells all of the high-quality ingredients you'd need for a luxurious feast.

#gourmetgroceries #expensivestuff

RESTAURANTS

C AL SULTAN BRAHIM

Starco, Minet El Hosn, Downtown
Telephone: +961 (0)1 989989
Daily from noon-12am

To feel like a sultan, one must eat at Sultan. With impeccable service – even suffocating at times – this upscale gem has the freshest fish in town. From squid, prawns, grouper, to red mullet, whether roasted, grilled, fried or raw, the choice is yours. The sea bream sashimi, served with a selection of spices and soy sauce is a specialty of theirs. To accompany your feast, try their spicy "Downtown *Hummus*", which gives an interesting kick to the traditional dip. As with most Lebanese restaurants, be prepared for an array of desserts to come your way without having ordered them (although we doubt you'll have any objections).

Tip: head over to the one in Jounieh, just on the outskirt of Beirut, for a beautiful view, incredible setting and for some fresh air.

Recommended dish: Sammak ras Asfour - lightly battered and fried fish cubes, marinated in a soy, lemon and coriander sauce – enjoy it 'cause it's expensive (LBP 75.000/50$ for 500g).

#dontcomewearingflipflops

D BALTHUS

Ghandour Bldg, French Av. Downtown
Telephone: +961 (0)1 371077
Daily from 12.30pm-3.30pm, 8pm-11.30pm

Beirut's fussiest unanimously choose Balthus as their favourite French bistro, as this deliciously expensive brasserie serves first-rate food in a beautiful interior. All the luxuries that could make you feel important are available, including foie gras, lamb gigot, oysters and an extensive wine-list. Do expect to pay up to LBP 120.000/80$ for your meal – excluding drinks.

E BRGR & CO

Patriarch Howayek St. Beirut Souks, Downtown
Telephone: +961 (01) 999 836
Daily from noon-12am

Londoners may have spotted this little jewel in the streets of Soho, but welcome to the original ones. Curated by super-chef Hussein Hadid, these meat-eries deliver gourmet burgers in open kitchens for all to impatiently crave. From spicy, fatty to "diet" burgers, you may take your pick.

Recommended dish: the Butcher's Cut, a burger made from the best cuts of meat (LBP 35.000/22$).

#parmesantrufflefries #threesizeburgers

F COCTEAU

Palladium Bldg, Park Ave, Downtown
Telephone: +961 (0)1 970707
Daily from 12.30pm-3.30pm, 8pm-11.15pm

French food is a favourite among the Lebanese, and they don't mess around. This remarkable upscale restaurant serves delectable dishes worthy of a Michelin star. As with most fantastic restaurants, Cocteau is unfortunately far from cheap and therefore won't be seeing us every day... their loss.

Recommended dish: salade gourmande de foie gras (LBP 32.000/22$).

#specialoccasions #youcantgowrongwithfrenchfood

G INDIGO ON THE ROOF

Le Gray Hotel, Martyrs' Sq, Downtown
Telephone: +961 (0)1 972000
Daily from 7.30am-11.30am, 12.30pm-3.30pm, 7.30pm-11.30pm

Lounged on the roof of Le Gray hotel, Indigo's got quite a few things to show off about: panoramic view, fine cuisine and excellent service, to name a few. Using the freshest ingredients of the Mediterranean, dishes such as the Seafood linguini with chili and lemon oil (LBP 36.000/24$) and the Thai baked sea bass in banana leaf (LBP 52.000/35$) are meticulously concocted to fit any fussy standards.

#michelinstarstandards

H KAMPAÏ

Ground Floor, Palladium Bldg, Rafic Salloum St.
Minet el Hosn
Telephone: +961 (0)1 999093
Daily from noon-12am

Japanese restaurants – scrap that – Asian restaurants are seldom good in this city. Kampaï is among the few that understand the refinement of the exotic cuisine, and doesn't push to "westernize" each dish. The spacious golden room is set around an open kitchen, allowing you to keep an eye out for funky dishes. If you like things hot and spicy yet soft and creamy, try the Fire Kampai Roll, (sesame sprinkled roll with octopus, squid, green tobico, mayo and 4 kinds of chilli. LBP 11.000/7.5$).

#trendysushi #yellowfever #sexandthecity

I MANDALOUN SUR MER

BIEL, Downtown
Telephone: +961 (0)1 999330
Daily from noon-12am

Located right below the infamous "Sky Bar" nightclub, this restaurant offers a beautiful view of Beirut's coastline. When the weather permits (which, let's be honest, happens most of the year), take a seat by the shore, enjoy the refreshing breeze and indulge in some outstanding fish. Seeing the bill may feel like torture, but the top-notch quality justifies the fee.

Tip: ask for the catch of the day, as it sets this place apart.

#fishwithaview

J MOMO AT THE SOUKS
Jewellery Souks, Downtown
Telephone: +961 (0)1 999767
Tuesday-Sunday from 7pm-11.30pm

By the same owner as London's famous Momo's and Sketch, this particular Momo looks over Beirut's Downtown souks (hence the name). With its dreamy outdoor terrace and Oriental indoor setting, this place offers enchanting food and interesting cocktails. Quality and taste are the basis of all their recipes. The fresh tomato gazpacho paired with a blackcurrant sorbet is delightful, but let's not forget their slightly spicy signature couscous tagine of lamb shoulder with grilled chicken skewers and real (!!) merguez sausages - excuse the enthusiasm but they are not easily found in this city.

Recommended dish: lobster cappuccino with cubes of caramelized mangos. (LBP 41.000/27$).

#hautecuisineenthusiasts #jetsetters #dinner

BARS

K IRIS
An-Nahar Building, Downtown
Telephone: +961 (0)3 090936
April-October Monday to Sunday from 6pm-2am

Summer in Beirut tends to go hand in hand with rooftop crazies. Iris may be a bit too "lets-pretend-we're-in-St-Tropez", but the view, the setting and the splendid cocktails make up for the somewhat superficial crowd. Order their porn-star martini, which is served with a shot of champagne on the side (might as well go all out and fit in, right? LBP 24.000/16$). Over the years waiters may have come and gone, but the service sadly seems to remain shit, so patience is key here, OR, do as we do and order your next 3 rounds in one go to be set – for a little while at least.

#welcometosainttropez #blingbling #drivingcadillacsinourdreams

K JULEP'S

Uruguay St. Downtown
Telephone: +961 (0)1 3 02 92 02
Daily from noon-2am

Located on a pedestrian alleyway, this teeny-weeny bar mixes some of the capital's best cocktails. Innovation is the mantra of the owners, who regularly travel for inspiration. The Elderberry tea gimlet, made of St Germain elderberry liquor, infused with tea and gin, is especially worth the detour. Their lavender and elderflower sour (with lemon juice and gin) are an original alternative to the good-old gin and tonic (LBP 17.000/11$). Feeling funky? Try their ruby red margarita, which is actually served in a grapefruit. We've never left this place sober.

#cocktailoftheweek #chillnight #gowiththeflow

A ruby red margarita at Julep's

ACHRAFIEH

- **A** Cannelle
- **B** Evasion
- **C** Ferme Saint Jacques
- **D** Ghattas
- **E** Hanna Mitri
- **F** House of Zejd
- **G** L'Atelier du Miel
- **H** Makari & Hachem
- **I** Makari & Hachem
- **J** Noura Pastry
- **K** Al Dente & Albergo Rooftop Hotel
- **L** Al Mayass
- **M** Bergerac
- **N** Boubouffe
- **O** Bread Republic
- **P** Kabab-Ji
- **Q** Margherita
- **R** Sô
- **S** Yasmina
- **T** Freiha
- **U** Furn Michel Saade
- **V** Zataar w Zeit

ACHRAFIEH

L ocated on a hill, Achrafieh is an upper class Christian residential area, which houses many shops, hotels and restaurants. The quarter was badly affected by the war, with rockets and bombs having damaged a substantial amount of its architectural heritage. The tearing down hasn't quite stopped, sadly, and authentic historical buildings are constantly being replaced by brand new ones. Lebanese law prohibits construction, or requires it to cease, on sites where archaeological remains are found. Many, however, choose to ignore this rule.

On a brighter note, the neighbourhood nevertheless has some splendid houses (especially in Sursock), and tasty gems.

SHOPS

A CANNELLE
SNA Bldg, General Fouad Chehab Ave, Tabaris, Achrafieh
Telephone: +961 (0)1 202169
Monday-Saturday from 8am-8pm; Sunday from 8am-6pm

Both a caterer and a patisserie, Cannelle is THE place to go for any sweet cravings. This pastry haven serves all the usuals and much much more. They're particularly proud of their chocolate gauffrettes but what they're essentially known for, all around Beirut, is their fucking amazing almond croissant (LBP 4.500/3$). Seriously, go try it now. Also good to know: you can order "Galette des Rois"

THE FOOD GUIDE: BEIRUT ON A PLATE

Canelle's famous croissants
aux amandes (p.85)

(King's cake) here all year round.

#weshoptoeat #almondcroissant #sweettooths #artyfood

B EVASION
Hospital saint George St. Achrafieh
Telephone: +961 (0)1 570099
Daily from 9am–9pm

Whether you're craving ice cream or chocolate, Evasion, as the name suggests, is the perfect escape from our pathetic calorie-counting hobby, so simply indulge. From the peach and lavender sorbets, the anise and cinnamon pralines to the salted caramel ganache, we're lovin' it. One kilo goes from LBP 30.000 to 60.000/20-40$.

#icecreamhelpsyoudigest

C FERME ST-JACQUES

Liban St. Achrafieh
Telephone: +961 (0)1 216076
Monday-Saturday from 10am-7pm

At St-Jacques, the selection of duck foie gras variants is as infinite as the farm chicken and duck aiguillettes are fresh. These products may all sound French to you, but they were all made in Lebanon at the owner's farm in Batroun. His goal was to prove that one doesn't need to be in France to prepare these culinary delicacies: mission accomplished.

#madeinlebanon #notforvegans #expensivestuff

D GHATTAS

Charles Malek Avenue, banks street, Achrafieh
Telephone: +961 (0)1 218 132
Odd opening hours, flexible but they unfortunately tend to close quite early

Hosting a party and want to feed your guests? Head over to Ghattas for miniature Lebanese delights. From mini Kibbeh and Manouche to small sized pastries, this caterer has it all. The spinach Fatayer and pumpkin Kibbeh are especially tasty. 12 spinach Fatayer for LBP 9.000/6$.

#minilebanesebites #sizedoesntmatter

🅔 HANNA MITRI

Mar Mitr St. Achrafieh
Telephone: +961 (0)1 322723
Monday-Saturday from 7.30am to whenever they feel like closing

Pardon our language, but this place really looks like shit. If you didn't know any better, you'd walk right past it without giving it a second glance - and you'd be making a terrible mistake. Ask anyone in Beirut what their favourite ice cream joint is and all, without any exception, will direct you here. Making ice cream since 1949, Hanna Mitri has perfected his scoops naturally thanks to a secret technique that doesn't require any artificial additives.

Recommended scoops: apricot with pine nuts or rose water sorbet (LBP 3.000/2$).

🐦 #ghettoicecream

🅕 HOUSE OF ZEJD

Mar Mitr St. - Ikariyat Georges Building, Achrafieh
Telephone: +961 (0)1 338003
Daily from 10am–8pm

This olive based shop sells everything from tapenade and olive oil to soap. All the produce is local and of the brand "Zejd", which means oil in the ancient Phoenician language. If you're looking for souvenirs to bring home, we highly recommend you drop by and discover their funky medleys of olive oils from sage, pomegranate, chilli and basil to orange (LBP 5000/3.33$ for 100ml).

🐦 #oliveoilisgoodforyou

Ⓖ L'ATELIER DU MIEL

Tabaris, Next to BLC Bank, Achrafieh
Telephone: +961 (0)1 322 064
Monday–Saturday from 10am-7pm

Welcome to Honey Land. This petite boutique sells their very own organic sweet elixir in different flavours; most of which are Lebanese excluding those only found in France, such as rosemary. From raspberry to the very Lebanese cedar-wood, the aromas here are rich. For a lighter taste try their oak honey (450g for LBP 30.000/19.5$). The owner also makes other charming honey-based products, like nougats, sweets, cakes, tea, sorbet and ice cream.

Tip from the shopkeeper: replace whatever you've been putting in your coffee with 1 tbsp of honey. It's sublime.

🐦 #honeymulledwine #getmeaspoon #hipsterboutique

Ⓗ LA BOULANGERIE BIO

In front of the Saint-Nicolas garden, Achrafieh
Telephone: +961 (0)1 334654
Monday-Friday from 8am-7pm ; Saturday from 8am-2pm

Wanna consume nasty-free bread? This bakery is your best solution. From their crusty baguettes and muffins, to the milk rolls and madeleines, everything is certified organic. Or just keep it simple and grab a "pain-aux-raisins" for breakfast before strolling around the city. Baguettes from LBP 3.000/2$.

🐦 #cantresistthesmellofhotbread

Ⓘ MAKARI & HACHEM

Near the mosque, Basta, Achrafieh
Telephone: +961 (0)1 643423
Daily from 10am-2pm

This *Furn* sells one thing and one thing only: *Moufataka*. What's that, you ask? It's a rice pudding with *Tahini*, turmeric and pine nuts, which requires hours of stirring. It may not sound appealing to you, but trust us, it is divine. The owner, Abou Omar, closes his store at 2pm as his babies are usually sold out by then.

#feelingmoufatakish #runfattyrun

Ⓙ NOURA PASTRY

Sassine Square, Achrafieh
Telephone: +961 (0)1 215806
Monday from 9am–8pm;
Tuesday-Sunday from 07.30am-8.30pm

Open for decades, this pastry shop also offers great catering services. Order their specialty, the "N by Noura", an extremely creamy and fondant chocolate cake (LBP 4.000/2.5$ for one piece), and ask for a few cheeky marrons glacés on the side!

#notliketheoneinlondon

RESTAURANTS

🅚 ALBERGO HOTEL ROOFTOP

Albergo Hotel, 137 Abdel Wahab El Inglizi St. Achrafieh
Telephone: +961 (0)1 339797
Daily from 9am-12am

Unlike most of Beirut's rooftops, the Albergo's isn't bling-bling. This Garden of Eden is one of the city's most pleasant spots to enjoy breakfast, lunch, tea or dinner. Their truffle scrambled eggs and mini burgers are devilishly good. To quench your thirst, order some of their homemade rose lemonade, which isn't on the menu but is definitely worth the hassle – especially if you sneakily mix it with vodka.

Recommended dish: Lebanese breakfast combo including: fried eggs sprinkled with *Sumac, Labneh, Halloumi*, honey from the Chouf mountains, thyme *Manouche* and fresh vegetables. (LBP 37.000/24$).

#lovers #boutiquehotelenthusiasts

K AL DENTE

Albergo Hotel, (ground floor) 137 Abdel Wahab El Inglizi St. Achrafieh
Telephone: +961 (0)1 202201

Sunday-Friday from 1pm-2am; kitchen closes at 11.30pm; Saturday from 8pm-11.30pm

As its name suggests, Al Dente's cuisine is done just right. This high-end restaurant – with it's just as high ceilings, chandeliers and velvet everything – is a real treat for haute-cuisine enthusiasts. Luckily, refined doesn't rhyme with boring here - so go ahead and order the rosemary and stuffed artichoke risotto seasoned with dry martini (LBP 33.000/22$), and thank us later.

#grownups #specialoccasions #thegodfatherwashere

🅛 AL MAYASS

Trabaud St. Achrafieh
Telephone: +961 (0) 1 215046
Daily from noon-12am

Lamb Kebab in sweet and sour cherry sauce at Al Mayass

Armenian food is quite popular in Beirut, and for good reason. This homely little restaurant offers some of the city's best dishes, which never fail to make us drool. Definitely don't miss out on their house-special *Basterma* Al Mayass (cured beef canapé topped with fried quail's eggs), or on their exceptional *Mouhammara* (sweet spicy red pepper paste with crushed walnuts). Desserts are not their forte, but the Asmaliyah Mayass (*Asmaliyah*, covered with cotton candy and seasoned with sugar syrup) may sound quite

White fish with ginger and lemon sauce at Bergerac

fatty, but is truly worth a try.

Tip: unless you're a big cheesy music fan, don't encourage the man strolling around with his guitar to sing because then he just won't stop.

Recommended dish: lamb *Kebab* in sweet and sour cherry sauce. (LBP 28.000/19$).

 #smallandcosy #orderthemanti #secondround

BERGERAC
Furn El Hayek St. Achrafieh
Telephone: +961 (0)1 330013
Tuesday-Saturday from noon-4pm, 8pm-11.30pm; Sunday from noon-4pm

This quaint little French "bistro du quartier" serves tasty dishes from the southwest region of France. If you can look past the rather obnoxious waiter, you'll see that the cuisine never fails.

Recommended dish: white fish with ginger and lemon sauce. (LBP 24.000/16$).

 #casuallunch #frenchalltheway

Ⓝ BOUBOUFFE

Charles Malek Avenue, Achrafieh
Telephone: +961 (0)1 200408
Daily from 8am-12.30am

Sheep tripe served every Sunday at Boubouffe

Although these gobblers were originally known for their appealing stuffed sheep tripe served every Sunday, they've now become tremendously famous for their gastro *Shawarma*s (LBP 8.000/5.33$) and fully loaded burgers, complete with fried egg!

#kitschandcosy #bestshawarmaintown

Ⓞ BREAD REPUBLIC

Furn El Hayek St. Achrafieh
Telephone: +961(0)1 201520
Daily from 7.30am-11pm

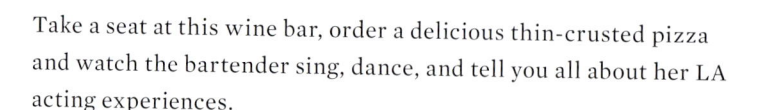

Take a seat at this wine bar, order a delicious thin-crusted pizza and watch the bartender sing, dance, and tell you all about her LA acting experiences.

P KABAB-JI

Alfred Naccache St. Achrafieh
Telephone: +961 (0)1 331133
Daily from 8am-12am

See review in Hamra & Clemenceau p.53

Q MARGHERITA

ABC Mall Level 3 Achrafieh
Telephone: +961 (0) 1 324 824
Daily from 12.30pm-12am

See review in Gemmayzeh & Saifi p.125

R SÔ

St Nicholas St. Achrafieh
Telephone: +961 (0)1 336644
Daily from noon-1am

For the past 15 years, Sô has managed to remain "in" with the upper class. The menu has barely changed since it opened, and serves international food, from pizza and sushi to frog legs and steak. The service is as top notch as the food is good.

#jetsetters #peoplewatchers #abitofeverything

S YASMINA
Akkawi St. Achrafieh
Telephone: +961 (0)1 206406
Monday–Sunday from 12.30pm-3.30pm; 8.30pm-11.30pm

For some good ol' Indian food, check out this funky restaurant set in a beautiful old Lebanese house. The menu includes all the expected dishes you'd find in an Indian restaurant outside of India, including their succulent butter chicken (LBP 37.000/25$). If there during the summer, their outdoor terrace is da-shizzle.

#indianfusion

STREET FOOD

T FALAFEL FREIHA
Madrassat Salam St. opposite ABC mall, Achrafieh
Telephone: +961 (0)1 321608
Daily from 10am-10pm

Since 1945, this 2-seater stall has been providing Beirutis with remarkable wraps. Their *Falafels* are made with fava beans and diners get to pick their seasoning between regular, sesame, spicy and unsalted.

#falafelsarecheap

FURN MICHEL SAADE
Moumne St. Achrafieh
Daily from 6.30am-2pm

All the variations of the tastiest of *Manouches* are served here, all you need to do is tell Michel exactly how you like yours.
We like our *Lahm bi Ajeen* with a thin crust, light on the meat, and seasoned with lemon and chilli powder. But that's just us. (LBP 2.000/1.3$ per Manouche).

#supercheap #bestkeptsecret

ZAATAR W ZEIT
ABC mall Achrafieh
Telephone: +961 (0)1 211711
Open 24/7

See review in Gemmayzeh & Saifi p.131

• MONNOT & SODECO •

- **A** Marzipan
- **B** Mikhael
- **C** Pâte à Choux
- **D** Rafic al Rashidi
- **E** Abdel Wahab
- **F** Al Falamanki
- **G** BRGR Co.
- **H** Café Sho
- **I** Em Sherif
- **J** Le relais de L'Entrecôte
- **K** Nonna
- **L** Sushi Bar
- **M** Yumi
- **N** Pacifico
- **O** Orfali
- **P** M. Shayoun vs Shayoun Falafel
- **Q** Empire Sodeco Cinema

MONNOT & SODECO

A busy area filled with shops and offices. Rue Monnot, which was named after a French Jesuite, Father Ambroise Monnot, is Sodeco's cutest and yummiest road. The one-way cobblestoned street includes an array of restaurants, shops, and bars, and used to be the "going out" area of Beirut, before being first replaced by Gemmayzeh, and then by Mar Mikhael.

SHOPS

A LE MARZIPAN
Museum Square, Adlieh, in the outskirt of Sodeco
Telephone: +961 (0)1 616896
Monday–Friday from 9am-6pm Saturday from 9am-2pm

Since 1965, this boutique has been making and selling the sweet almond paste based on a family recipe. On top of the classic marzipan, almond and cinnamon macaroons, among other pastries, have been added to the menu.

B MIKHAEL

Monnot St. Monnot
Telephone: +961 (0)1 327 226
Monday-Saturday from 8am-5pm

Proudly open since 1929, Mikhael specializes in milky pleasures. The boutique sells fresh *Laban, Labneh* and even *Laban*-based soaps! For breakfast or dessert, take a seat and order their *Areesh and Kashta* (each LBP 6.000/4$) with honey. The dishes' light and condensed texture glides on your tongue as the sweet honey thrills your palate.

#cheeselovers #notforlactoseintolerants

Areesh with honey

🅒 PÂTE À CHOUX

Sodeco St. Sodeco
Telephone: +961 (0)1 614150
Monday-Friday from 8.30am-8.30pm ;Saturday from 8.30am-7pm ; Sunday from 9.30am-4pm

Come and indulge (or the other way around) in some shamefully scrumptious cakes and pastries. Don't expect the fresh fruit tart or healthy banana bread types here, instead get the upsettingly addictive Nutella cake to share (LBP 70.000/46$-it's a big cake) or Nutella tart if you're a loner or if your friends just don't get it. (Note: you may want to call ahead to order the Nutella cake, it's clearly quite popular)

🐦 #thesweeterthebetter #foodissex #nutellaoverdose

🅓 RAFIC AL RASHIDI

Monnot St. Monnot
Telephone: +961 (0)1 398800
Daily from 7am-9pm

Famous for their *Knefe* served every morning until 11am, Rafic makes a great stop for morning promenades.

🐦 #goeasyonthesyrup

RESTAURANTS

🅔 ABDEL WAHAB
51 Abdel Wahab El Inglizi St. Monnot
Telephone: +961 (0)1 200550
Daily from noon-12am

This classic Lebanese joint has become a trademark and is actually named after the street it was built on. As the ultimate spot to munch on some gourmet food without slaughtering your wallet (meal for two with drinks LBP 70.000/50$), Abdel Wahab has evidently become a favourite among the Lebanese. Although everything on the menu may be expected, it is beyond delicious.

#3hourmezzesession #openairterrace

🅕 AL FALAMANKI
Damascus Rd, Sodeco
Telephone: +961 (0)1 323456
Daily 24hours

The first thing you should know about this spacious spot is that it's open 24/7, meaning that it's the ideal hangout for post-party cravings. Decked as an actual home, the décor is authentic with lots of little objects here and there, unmatched chairs and a dreamy garden filled with fairy lights and narguileh smoke. Regulars vary from older men playing board games to inebriated adolescents. Its Lebanese Mezze remains honest, cheap and tasty. *Hummus* LBP 8.000/5.5$.

#hipsters #drunks #lovers #fools #everyone

G BRGR & CO
Abdel Wahab St. Sodeco
Telephone: +961 (01) 333 511
Sunday-Saturday from noon-12am

See review in Downtown p.78

H CAFÉ SHO
304 Monnot St. Monnot
Telephone: +961(0)1 424051
Monday-Saturday from noon-12am

A personal favourite of ours, this humbly cute eatery brings Asian food to a whole other level. The dishes are fresh and simple with creative twists. For small appetites, try one of their summer rolls; the fillings are funky from chicken and mango, to duck and avocado. All other dishes come in gigantic portions, we're talking impossible-not-to-spill-some-on-the-table-cause-its-so- big gigantic. Their concept is easy, from the enormous black board you pick: your main dish (the selection goes from curry chicken skewers, sweet chilli fish, pineapple and beef teriyaki to duck with lemongrass) and your side (rice with peanuts, vegetable rice, curry noodles, ratatouille, or potatoes) – AND the assortment comes with a veg / fruit salad. Want to add a lil' somethin'? Their counter bestows a huge selection of sauces for every taste. Thursdays are Thai days, and a little birdie told us that their pad thai was to die for.

Recommended dish: the caramelized prawn skewers (LBP 25.000/16.5$).

#healthfreakswhohappentoalsobefatschweins

EM SHERIF
Victor Hugo St. Monnot
Telephone: +961 (0)1 207207
Daily from 12.30am-4pm, 8.30pm-12am

The décor might be extremely overdone, in an "I'm rich but have no taste" kind of way, but the Lebanese-meets-Syrian food they serve is so lusciously wonderful that you will enjoy every single second of this trippy experience. First off, there's no menu here, but a fixed price of LBP 90.000/60$ per person (for dinner; LBP 55.000/36$ for lunch) which gets you what seems like an unlimited number of dishes. Pace yourself though, as it's only when you think you

A feast at Em Sherif

couldn't possibly eat another bite that they'll bring out the mains.

Recommended dishes: it's a set menu but watch out for the *Fattoush* salad (their dressing makes it one of the best we've ever had).

🐦 #peoplewholiketofeelimportant #bringiton #eattilyoudrop

🟢 J LE RELAIS DE L'ENTRECÔTE
Khoury Bldg, Abdel Wahab El Inglizi St. Monnot
Telephone: +961(0)1 332087
Daily from 12.30pm-3.30pm; 7.30pm-11.30pm

No menu. 1 salad starter, chunks of beef entrecôte drowned in a fucking amazing secret sauce and all this served with fries. Amen. (LBP 60.000/40$).

Café gourmand

Recommended dish: café gourmand for dessert - literally served with 3 huge chunks of delicious cakes and a scoop of vanilla ice cream.

🐦 #steakparade #neversaynotofries

Ⓚ NONNA
Abdel Wahab El Inglizi St. Monnot
Telephone: +961 (0)1 333082
Daily from 12.30pm-11.30pm

Pizza Formaggi

This one's for those who like their pizzas thin, and we're talking paper-thin. The crust is a perfect balance of crispy and crunchy and the toppings just melt in your mouth. Bonus point: if you're on a diet, some pizzas can be served with a hole in the middle filled with rocket salad.

Recommended pizza: the formaggi (LBP 24.750/16.50$).

 #sickoflebanesefood

L SUSHI BAR ($$$$)
Abdel Wahab El Inglizi St. Monnot
Telephone: +961 (0)1 338555
Daily from 12.30pm-4pm, 8pm-11.30pm

When this restaurant first opened, they had to give out free meals for 3 months as the food was that bad. They've come a long way since then. Let's skip the décor description, as you can just imagine it seeing the 4-dollar bar sign above. Their dishes are – for the most part – sublime, so let us help you order the right ones. Although the sushi is very fresh and respectable, don't waste too much of your appetite on it as the real deal is the exceptional black cod and the incomparable lamb served in miso butter. Yes, lamb is far from being Japanese, but you won't mind that when you feel the meat melting in your mouth and you experience a lip-smacking food orgasm.

Favourite dish: see above, obviously.

 #richpeople

YUMI
Monnot St. Monnot
Telephone: +961 (0)1 337838
Daily from 7pm-1.30am

This little sushi lounge decked on a tiny alleyway opposite Pacifico (read below), makes beautiful cocktails and pretty delicious rolls. The spiced Sakerina, (ginger, lychee, brown sugar and sake) and majestic eel maki roll (eel with tempura covered shrimps and caramelized mangoes, LBP 18.500/12$ for 4 pcs) made us tingle with delight.

#foraperfectdate

BARS

PACIFICO
Monnot St. Monnot
Telephone: +961 (0)1 204446
Daily 7pm-1.30am. Happy Hour 7pm-8pm

Pacifico is Beirut's original Tex-Mex restaurant – at least that's the word on the street. Since then, many of its former employees have moved on and opened their own "cantinas" based on this cocktail dreamland, but for most Pacifico remains "the one". The food isn't bad and can even be quite good at times, but their Margaritas are always spot on, so best to make it a pre or post-dinner visit.

#tequilamakesushappy #cheers #alwayshappening

STREET FOOD

⊙ ORFALI
Petro Trad St. Sodeco
Telephone: +961 (0)1 505072
Daily from 10am-12am Delivery available

Original Lebanese wraps and *Kebabs*, ready to go. Sandwiches are freshly prepared right in front of your eyes. The Armenian inspired little *Kibbeh* balls filled with sweet cherries are especially good (LBP 1.500/1$ a piece) and so are the cucumber *Laban Ayran* (LBP 3.500/2.5$) or the funky blackberry *Arak* (LBP 4.500/3$) to quench your thirst.

Recommended wrap: *Kebab bil Jibne* (lamb and cheese *Kebab* served with avocado and *Hummus* sauce) LBP 6.500/4.5$

#funkydecor #mooo

M. SAHYOUN VS. SAHYOUN FALAFEL

Maliyeh Bldg, Damascus Rd, Sodeco
Telephone: +961 (0)1 633188
Monday–Saturday from 10am–11pm

These two almost identical holes-in-the-wall are known to sell the best *Falafel* in town. Rumour has it that the Sahyoun family originally only held one but after the father passed away, the two brothers split up – literally. One inherited the outlet and the other opened his own right next door. Gossip aside, both offer the perfect cure to a hangover: a deliciously hearty Falafel sandwich.

#cheapasfuck #falafelfever #pickyourfavourite

FOOD ACTIVITY

🅠 EMPIRE SODECO CINEMA
Sodeco Sq, Sodeco
Telephone +961 (0)1 616707
www.empirepremiere.com

Fancy watching a film on a lazy-boy, your head pressed against a comfy pillow, tucked in a soft blanket, sipping on your favourite cocktail AND nibbling on some sushi from the Sushi Bar restaurant? We thought so. Regular ticket LBP 30.000/20$; excluding food & drinks.

#lazymotherfuckers #highrollers

Orfali (p.112)

GEMMAYZEH & SAIFI

- **A** Souk El Tayeb
- **B** Balima
- **C** Burgundy
- **D** Em Nazih
- **E** Ginette
- **F** Joanna's table at Kitsch
- **G** Kobe
- **H** La Centrale
- **I** Le Chef
- **J** Margherita Pizzeria 
- **K** Mayrig Restaurant
- **L** Petit Gris
- **M** Dragonfly
- **N** Joe Pena's
- **O** Kayan
- **P** Torino Express
- **Q** Fern Ghattas
- **R** Makhlouf Cocktail
- **S** Zataar w Zeit
- **T** Kitchen Lab

GEMMAYZEH & SAIFI

Gemmayzeh, also known as the artistic bohemian district, is a popular Christian neighbourhood, which consists of narrow streets filled with art galleries, restaurants, cafes and bars. Its main street, "rue Gouraud", was actually named after General Henri Gouraud, during the French colonial period, and oozes a certain European *"je ne sais quoi"*. Gemmayzeh can get quite packed, so avoid travelling around by car, as you'll most definitely get stuck in traffic. Instead, go for the pedestrian option; though be prepared to be incessantly honked at by hopeful taxi drivers

Walk towards Downtown, cross the horrendous highway-looking street where the traffic lights are close to useless and you will get to delightful **Saifi Village**. This teeny weeny residential neighbourhood stops at the beginning of the former green line (which used to separate the Muslim quarters from the Christian ones during the Lebanese Civil war). Built and maintained by the private company Solidere, the village is fairly quiet and extremely pleasant for a brief escape.

MARKETS

Ⓐ SOUK EL TAYEB
Debbas Square, Saifi Village
Telephone: +961 (0)1 989041
Saturday 4pm-8pm

See review in Downtown p.75

RESTAURANTS

Ⓑ BALIMA
Ghalghoul St. Saifi Village
Telephone: +961 (0)1 985295
Daily from 8am-12pm

Located in a cute Hollywood-meets-Disney looking neighbourhood, Balima sadly lacks buzz and clientele. The simple menu with fresh vegetables from the farmer's market of Souk el Tayeb (see above) isn't to be blamed though. From the creamy chicken alfredo fusilli (LBP 31.000/21$), to the curry beef (LBP 33.000/22$), the food's spot on.

#retro #noisehaters

Balima

BURGUNDY

752 Gouraud St. Gemmayzeh
Telephone: +961 (0)1 999820
Monday-Friday from noon-4pm, 8pm-12am; Saturday 8pm-12am

High-end, yet not flashy bling-bling, this gastronomic jewel has a beautiful selection of wine and food (to switch them 'round for once). Their French medleys are always refined and served like pieces of art on a plate. The prices are sadly just as grand as the cuisine.

Recommended dish: the slightly grilled wagyu fillet MB9 LBP 189.000/125$ (but the MB6 is just as wow LBP 99.000/65$)

#richpeople #hautecuisinelovers #winebar

D EM NAZIH

Pasteur St. Gemmayzeh
Telephone: +961 (0)1 562509
Daily from 8am-4am

Thrillingly cheap, yet charmingly authentic, Em Nazih is where you'll find many expats chilling and boozing. This self-service restaurant serves those homely dishes, usually made by Lebanese mothers and not really found in restaurants. Typical Mezze are still an option though, if you like to stick to what you know.

Recommended dish: one of the 4-5 dishes of the day, found on the wall next to the counter. Wednesday night is quiz night, if you're up for some serious competition. *Hummus* is around LBP 4.000/2.5$.

#urbangarden #touristsandlocalhipsters #noservice

E GINETTE

Convivium V Project, Gouraud St. Gemmayzeh
Telephone: +961 (0)1 570440
Daily from 8am-10pm

Drawing inspiration from "Colette" in Paris, Ginette is a hip and spacious café-restaurant concept store. On top of being an easy hangout spot for the free Wi-Fi and boutique, the food is honestly banging. From Nutella waffles (LBP 10.000/7$) with fresh pomegranate juice (LBP 8.000/4.5$) for breakfast, healthy salads or hot dog paninis (LBP 10.000/7$) for lunch to banana cream pie or creamy cheesecake with blueberry sauce for teatime, we've never been let down.

#fashionistas #unaffordableshop

JOANNA'S TABLE AT KITSCH
Germanos Bldg, 14 Gemmayzeh St. Gemmayzeh
Telephone: +961 (0)1 575075
Daily from 8am-9pm

In Beirut, one grows.... sideways. Joanna offers a great escape for the skinnies or wannabe-skinnies, in a charming boutique. Using only fresh ingredients from her father's farm, her plates can be gulped down guilt-free. The menu fluctuates; dishes can vary from a crunchy green salad (LBP 18.000/12$), fish curry with rice

Thai chicken salad at Joanna's Table

(LBP 25.000/17$) to fresh shrimp dim sum (LBP 3.000/2$ each). Diet-haters, no need to "next" this one just yet, the desserts are oddly stuffing and devilishly tempting. While waiting, take a chance to wander around the funky concept-store; you're bound to find something.

#cuteasabutton #friendly #theladies

G KOBE
Pasteur St. Gemmayzeh
Telephone: +961 (0)1 561016
Daliy from 12.30pm-12.30am

Hopefully, by the time you read this, the place won't have shut down. The sad thing about this city is that most people will only go to restaurants that have been recommended to them by others. The Lebanese aren't very keen on trying new things. Kobe, unfortunately, has been affected by that and neglected. If you don't mind dining in an empty restaurant with flawless service while enjoying some really good New York-esque Japanese style sushi (LBP 9.000-23.000/6- 15$), dim sum (LBP 7.000-23.000/4.5-15$) and teppanyaki, made with market-fresh ingredients, then voila!

#peoplearemissingout #creativesushi

LA CENTRALE

Mar Maroun Church St. Saifi
Telephone: +961 (0)1 575858
Daily from 8pm-12.30am

Aside from the fact that the crowd is slightly pompous and that prices are excruciatingly high, Centrale offers a beautiful setting, with both indoor and outdoor seating depending on the season. The French and Italian fused food is truly magnificent. The foie gras (LBP 44.000/29$) made us want to order 3 more and the scallop ceviche (LBP 35.000/23$) made us regret having ordered the foie gras. You get the drill. Check out its funky upstairs tube-bar for some very good drinks. If you are counting the pennies, skip dinner and head straight to the bar.

#romanticplaceforfriends #quirkylift

🟠 LE CHEF

Gouraud St. Gemmayzeh
Telephone: +961 (0)1 445373
Monday-Saturday from 7am-12am

Extremely popular among expats, and not so much among locals, this modest restaurant prepares tasty homey Lebanese dishes. Don't be alarmed by the lack of native clientele, it's simply because they get to eat this type of food every weekend when they visit their aunt/grand-mother/mother's home – and we don't. The owner will most probably scream "welcome!" At you every 10 minutes, it's part of the experience…!

Tip: if you're not that hungry, know that they also do half-prices for half-portions. A full meal will still be around LBP 10.000/7$

🐦 #cheapestingemmayzeh #frenchhandwrittenmenu #localbeer

🟠 MARGHERITA

Gouraud St. Gemmayzeh
Telephone: +961 (0)1 560480
Daily from 12.30pm-12am

Margherita is arguably the best pizzeria in town, and indisputably the most consistent. Served extra thin, their pizzas come in all shapes and flavours. Don't dismiss the pasta though, as the gnocchi con burrata e pomodorini (LBP 28.500/19$) is quite something. At the end of your meal, you're asked to pick a number between 1 and 90; choose the lucky draw and it's on the house.

Recommended dish: pizza Norcina (Mozzarella di bufala, truffle cream, truffle oil, mushrooms and black truffles LBP 46.000/30.50$)

🐦 #aintthatcheap #noreservation #friendsandfamily

🟡 K MAYRIG

Mansour Bldg, 282 Pasteur St. Gemmayzeh
Telephone: +961 (0)1 572121
Daily from noon-12am

Started by two cousins, Mayrig oozes warmth and is definitely great for family lunches or friendly dinners. Although you'll find similar dishes here as in most Armenian joints in town, their pepper paste (LBP 11.000/7.5$) and Manti (LBP 23.000/15.5$) carry the prize.

🐦 #bringyoursweatpants

🟡 L PETIT GRIS

Nahr Brahim St. Gemmayzeh
Telephone: +961 (0)1 443737
Monday 12.30pm-3.30pm; Tuesday-Sunday 12.30pm-3.30pm, 8.30pm-12am

French name, French décor and French food: welcome to Petit Gris. This slightly overpriced bistro, (beware, mains are LBP 37.000/25$ and above), tastes like Paris on a plate. Serving one of the best steak tartares in town, their dishes remain sweet and simple.

GEMMAYZEH & SAIFI

127

Jumbo shrimps with linguine, vegetables and a beautiful secret sauce at Petit Gris

The grilled veal cutlet with shiitake and potato wedges is quite a treat, especially when paired with their own brand of wine. Bon app'!

Recommended dish: jumbo shrimps with linguine, vegetables and a beautiful secret sauce. LBP 48.000/32$

#lepetitgrisisatypeofsnail

BARS

M DRAGON FLY
Gouraud St. Gemmayzeh
Telephone: +961 (0)1 561112
Daily from 6pm-2am. Happy hour 6pm-8pm

One of Gemmayzeh's oldest spots, Dragonfly never ceases to attract crowds and remains "in". The bartenders, who are dressed like barbers, meticulously prepare sumptuous cocktails, making sure they are just right.

Recommended drink: cocktail of the week (as it usually contains seasonal fruits; around LBP 15.000/10$)

#pitstopdrinks #ninothebartender #brieandapricotpizza

N JOE PENA'S
Hnneine Bldg, Boutros Dagher St. Gemmayzeh
Telephone: +961 (0)1 449906
Daily from 6.30pm-2am

Although this is a restaurant, we'd much rather recommend it for its swanky margaritas than meh Mexican food. Order them by the pitcher as the more, the merrier!

#meeeeeexiiicccoooooooooooo!!!

🟠 KAYAN
Lebnan St. Gemmayzeh
Telephone: +961 (0)3 899213
Daily from 5pm-2am

Friendly bartenders will guide you to an enchanting drunken world. This gastro-bar offers tasty simple nibbles and sublime complex cocktails.

Recommended drink: ask the bartender to make you his favourite (LBP 15.000/10$)

🐦 #goodstart #goodending #expensiveifyoukeepdrinking

🟠 TORINO
Express Gouraud St. Gemmayzeh
Telephone: +961 (0)3 611 456
Daily from 10am-late

Café by day and bar by night, this tiny spot is filled with character. With its unpretentious crowd and roughed up boho-chic décor, Torino makes the perfect pit stop between dinner and clubbing, or even clubbing and bedtime. The bartenders are big drinkers themselves, so know exactly how drinks should be served - and if you're lucky, they may even give out free shots at the end of the night (don't push for it though, we said if you're lucky).

Recommended drink: Russian Mojito (LBP 12.000/8$).

🐦 #comeasyouare #startservingboozeat11am #institution

STREET FOOD

🅠 FERN GHATTAS
Gouraud St. Gemmayzeh
Telephone: +961 (0)1 585218
Monday-Friday from 8am-3pm, Saturday from 7am-2pm, Sunday from 7am-1pm

With more than 30 different *Manouches* (LBP 1.500-4.500/1-3$) to choose from, Ghattas is a great spot for a cheap snack. Word on the street is that it serves the best traditional Lebanese pizzas in town. The Financial Times has even voted it one of the best local eateries.

🐦 #eatonthego #lebanesebakery

🅡 MAKHLOUF COCKTAIL
Gouraud St. Gemmayzeh
Telephone: +961 (0)1 575656
Daily from 10am-10pm
(they also deliver nearby)

If you're walking around Gemmayzeh or making your way Downtown for some serious shopping, take a quick stop here for some tasty thirst-quenchers. Juices are fresh and sometimes mixed with milk, honey and raw almonds for an Oriental cocktail. Create your own combo or ask to take a look at the secret menu behind the counter for some funkier options.

Recommended drink: strawberry and avocado juice. They add sugar and honey, so if you don't like it too sweet just tell them " balla seuker ". They'll get it. (LBP 6.000/4$).

#healthfreaks #fruitlovers #needvitamins

S ZAATAR W ZEIT
Gouraud St. Gemmayzeh
Telephone: +961 (0) 1 566471
Open 24/7

This Lebanese fast food chain is most definitely where you'll find us munching like pigs after a big night out. Zaatar w Zeit, which literally translates as thyme and oil, specializes in *Manouche*: the Middle-Eastern version of a thin pizza, with beautiful toppings ranging from spiced minced-beef (LBP 4.500/3$) to *Halloumi* and bacon (LBP 8.500/6$). Whether you eat in, take out, or get delivery, your wallet will love you – unlike your butt.

Recommended dish: *Manouche* - topped to your liking.

#cheapmunch #hangoverfood #24hours
#butalsohavequinoasalad

FOOD ACTIVITY

🅣 KITCHEN LAB
St Nicolas Stairs, Gouraud St. Gemmayzeh
Telephone: +961 (0)1 587 870
www.facebook.com/kitchenlablebanon

There are those who love eating food, and then there are those who are obsessed with every single thing about it. We're definitely food-stalkers ourselves, and Kitchen Lab is the sort of place we dream of at night. This organic grocery / stylish cooking accessories shop / cooking class centre is our type of sex shop. Classes teach cuisine from all over the world, so check their Facebook page to catch one that suits you.

Recommended to anyone who has already used "orgasmic" when describing food.

#foodporn

Kitchen Lab

• MAR MIHKAEL •

- **A** Oslo
- **B** Epicery
- **C** Frosty Palace
- **D** Happy Prince
- **E** L'humeur du Chef
- **F** Les Fenêtres
- **G** Marinella Trattoria
- **H** Mó restaurant
- **I** Seza Bistro Arménien
- **J** Tavolina 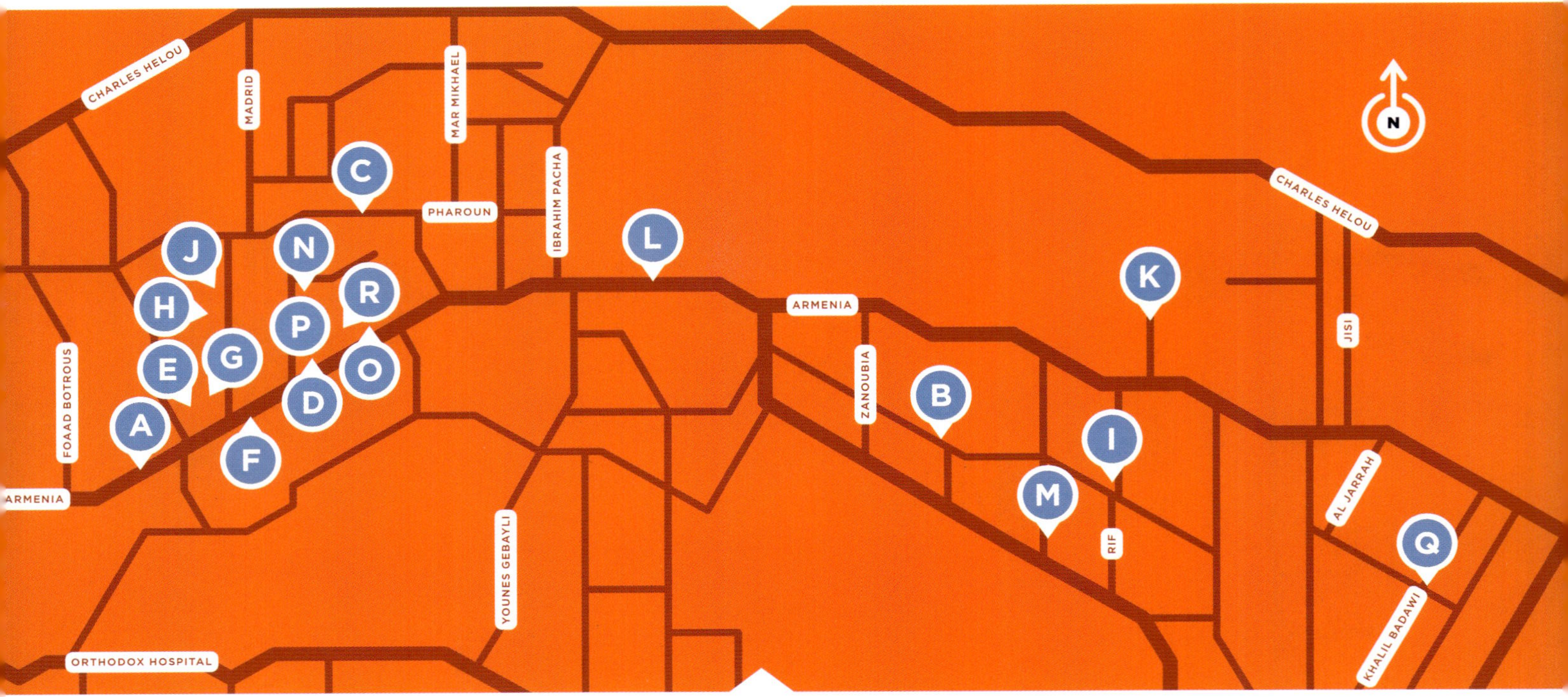
- **K** Tawlet
- **L** Toto's
- **M** Villa Clara
- **N** Anise
- **O** Central Station
- **P** Dictateur
- **Q** Internazionale
- **R** Vyvyan's

MAR MIKHAEL

Mar Mikhael, aka hipster-central, is Beirut's equivalent to Soho. The buzzing neighbourhood is filled with restaurants, bars, and galleries, yet was originally known as a more industrial hub. Walk all the way down and you will reach a bridge marking the beginning of Bourj Hammoud.

SHOPS

Ⓐ OSLO
Armenia St. Mar Mickhael
Telephone: +961 (0)1 576464
Monday–Friday from 9am–4pm Saturday from 9am–1.30pm Delivery Service Available

Located on a buzzing street, this unbearably cute bakery-meets-ice-cream parlour will lure you in within seconds. The funky selection of products makes it very difficult to choose between Nestlé milk and crème brulée ice cream, not to mention pomegranate sorbet, and we're ashamed to say we've uncontrollably tried them all. Their homemade Oreo cookies and Rose green Tea cake (LBP 24.000/16$) were unfortunately also victims of our gourmandise. The enchanting owner, Nayla Audi, is particularly fond of her salted caramel ice cream.

🐦 #madeinheaven #littlepieceofcandyinbeirut

Biscuits and cakes at Oslo (p.135)

RESTAURANTS

B EPICERY

Patriarche arida St. Mar Mikhael
Telephone: +961 76 046 556
Tuesday-Sunday 7pm-1am

With "drinks, food and spices" as their motto, Epicery really is the place to go for a spicy drunken night. Take a seat under the vineyards on the terrace, or in the minimalist modern décor, dig into their exquisite Changshu chicken salad (LBP 18.000/12$), glazed shrimps with saffron carrot purée (LBP 32.000/21$) or pineapple ravioli (LBP 15.000/10$) for dessert, but most of all get yourself a fucking drink. Sako, the head bartender, is a cocktail god and could really give New York or London's top mixologists some competition.

#secretgarden #themorethemerrier

C FROSTY PALACE

Pharaoh St. Mar Mikhael
Telephone: +961 (0)1 449595
Monday–Saturday from 11am-11pm

There's nothing better than a juicy burger and a good milkshake to cure a hangover. This tiny American diner not only plays great retro tunes but also serves some of best fatty sandwiches, burgers, pancakes, or desserts you'd want to chew on after a rough night or a good smoke. Salads are also available if your significant other sadly happens to be on a diet.

Recommended dish: the hoisin burger (it's a special, so fingers crossed) and the oreo milkshake (total for around LBP 40.000/26$).

🐦 #fatschweins #hangovers #munchies #dietisdiewithaT

ⓓ HAPPY PRINCE
Alexander Flemming St. Mar Mikhael
Telephone: +961 (0)1 569040
No reservations unless 6 or more. Daily from noon-3am

Decorated to look like a church, this joint is definitely not without sin. Accountable for most of our extra pounds, Happy Prince sure knows how to make us happy. Serving the absolute best meat in town, their burger is to die for. For Brunch, try their selection of

Steak and eggs sandwich

Bloody Marys and their Nutella Hot Coco (LBP 10.000/7$) with the steak and eggs sandwich (LBP 30.000/20$). But really, order the burger (LBP 23.000/15$).

#burgerandcocktail #happiestprince

E L'HUMEUR DU CHEF

Azirian Bldg, Armenia St. Mar Mikhael
Telephone: +961 (0)1 565495
Monday-Saturday from 12.30pm-3.30pm, 8pm-11pm

This little eatery's name literally translates as the chef's mood, meaning we can't guarantee you'll have a great meal as it depends on whether the chef got laid or not. Jokes aside, this one's got skills. The set menu changes daily and consists of a starter, a salad, a main and a dessert – with a vegetarian option always available (LBP 45.000/30$).

Tip for picky people: you can check out their Facebook page for a sneak peak, as they often share their daily menu.

#goodmoodgoodfood #foodadventure

F LES FENÊTRES

Armenia St. Mar Mikhael
Telephone: +961 (0)1 577578
Daily from noon-12am

Aside from the setting, which truly feels like a stereotypical movie set of what every foreigner believes France to be like - Les Fenêtres is doing a pretty good job at keeping foodies happy. As one of the

THE FOOD GUIDE: BEIRUT ON A PLATE

Raclette omelette

few outdoor spots to serve a good weekend brunch, we recommend you take your hungover self out here, for a good old raclette omelette (LBP 22.000/15$) or fish and chips (LBP 39.000/26$). For the more sophisticated ones among us, moules-frites and oysters (LBP 110.00/74$ for 12) are also ready to be devoured. Brunch is really just a suggestion though, you should go whenever.

#elegantlychilled #charlesbaudelaire

MARINELLA TRATTORIA
Madrid St. Mar Mikhael
Telephone: +961 (0)1 442342
Monday to Saturday from noon-4pm

Only open for lunch, this cutie-pie spot mostly attracts an older and more refined crowd. The ingredients are fresh and come straight from Italy – including the vegetables. Unlike most Italian restaurants, pizza ain't on the menu. No biggie though, as you'll clearly find something else to your liking. From the free-nibbles (standard and extra spicy saucisson – for the tough ones), to the selection of homemade pasta, we truly have no complaints. The daily specials never fail to impress but the scaloppini al limone with its butter-lemon sauce, sautéed potatoes and mushrooms is amazeballs.

Recommended dish: linguini langoustini (LBP 38.000/25$).
#lamamadeitalia #notcheapforlunch

MÓ
Madrid St. Mar Mikhael
Telephone: +961 (0)1 569 717
Sunday-Friday from 3pm-11.30pm ;
Saturday from noon-11.30pm

Representative of its name, this joint is small – but who said size mattered? Mó is on site, ready to answer your questions and to serve you like a prince. His menu is based on using local produce with a dash of originality. The juicy pork burger, with apples, caramelized onions and Gruyère may be heavy, but is definitely worth the bloat. The seafood couscous tagine is as refreshingly different as the fig duck fillet is toothsomely rich.

Recommended dish: Kan Kan Quinoa (spiced beef, with cinnamon, peanut butter, served with a Quinoa salad and guacamole) LBP 30.000/20$.

#didyousaypork? #schweinforschwein #hipsterhangout

SEZA

Patriarch Arida St. Mar Mikhael
Telephone: +961 (0)1 570711
Tuesday-Sunday from noon-4pm and 8pm-12am

Welcome to Seza! A cute and romantic Armenian bistro nestled on the ground floor of a beautiful old Lebanese home. Serving small to medium sized sharing platters of all of the usual Armenian delights, this is the ideal location for lovers to gaze into each other's eyes. Larger groups can order a selection of 15 dishes to share, with dessert and open Arak & beer, for LBP 50.000/33$.

#datenights #alittletreasure

J TAVOLINA

Kamille Youssef Chamoun St. Mar Mikhael
Telephone: +961 (0)1 442244
Daily from 12.30pm-11.30pm

On a side street off Mar Mikhael, this charismatic Italian really hits the spot. Serving thin wood-oven pizzas, creamy risottos, mouth-watering pasta and hearty meat dishes, you're bound to find a winner. We honestly have no complaints - except for the tacky plastic crowd, but that's a detail we can easily overlook.

Recommended dish: truffled raviolini (LBP 24.000/15$).

#moremangiare #glutenfreepasta #dailycheeseplateselection

K TAWLET SOUK EL TAYEB

Armenia St. Mar Mikhael
Telephone: +961 (0)1 448129
Monday-Friday from 1pm-4pm

Tawlet's dessert counter

THE FOOD GUIDE: BEIRUT ON A PLATE

Worth every single penny, Tawlet's concept is very special. Every day a different local chef prepares dishes from his specific region of Lebanon, using only the freshest ingredients, which are then presented on a buffet (LBP 50.000/33$ including unlimited *Arak*). We have never been disappointed here, and the beauty is that each visit is a new discovery of the country. The owner himself can be found smiling while devouring the food daily, and that's always a good sign!

Tawlet also caters for private dinners where you can attend cooking lessons in a group of 4 and more, to then enjoy your hard labour. Call to inquire.

#writingthismadeushungry

Tawlet's buffet

L TOTO'S

Armenia St. Mar Mikhael
Telephone: +961 (0)1 566991
Daily from noon-3.30pm, 8pm-11.30pm

Mar Mikhael is filled with Italian places. Toto's is definitely one of the most affordable yet delectable options. The decoration is rather kitsch, but the food is worth the headache. Their Lebanese pizza (LBP 24.000/16$) brings an interesting edge to the Italian delicacy and the uovo de Sophie (crispy organic poached egg with mushrooms and parmesan. LBP 20.000/17.5$) is a must.

Recommended dish: green asparagus cappellini with white truffle oil (LBP 29.000/19.50$). Or choose any pizza you want and it will be served 1-meter long for LBP 75.000/50$.

#fortheloveofitaly

M VILLA CLARA

Khenchara St. Mar Mikhael
Telephone: +961 (0)1 566898
Café open daily from 8am-1am, restaurant open daily from noon-3pm, 8pm-1am

Despite the Italian ring to its name, Villa Clara is very much French. This charming boutique hotel's café serves excellent cuisine in an enchanting old building. Most ingredients are organic and come straight out of their vegetable garden in the mountains or are bought daily at local markets. Spoil yourself with their not-so-cheap but spectacular steak tartare (LBP 79.000/53$) which is fastidiously prepared by the chef at your table. To finish off, have their raspberry meringue. We know, meringue aren't really our thing either, but here it comes fruity, soft and creamy yet crunchy; plus the portions are huge so ideal to share and fight over.

Tip: have a drink before getting the bill, it will soothe the pain.

#datenights #grownups #bellydancerwednesdaynights #nutellagauffre

Asparagus salad with Parma ham at Villa Clara

BARS

🅝 ANIS
Alexander Flemming St. Mar Mikhael
Telephone: +961 (0)1 70 977 926
Daily from 6pm-1.30am

Though we're strictly judging on food and drinks, this place really does deserve a few lines dropped in about its quaint, non-pretentious speakeasy décor. Done. With its extensive variety of homemade Arak and interesting house cocktails, Anise is ideal for pre-dinner drinks, date nights or for that drink you sometimes often just need.

Recommended drink: sage Margarita (if on the menu LBP 15.000/10$).

🐦 #sharplookingbartenders #jazzy

🅞 CENTRAL STATION
Armenia St. Mar Mikhael
Telephone: +961 71 736737
Daily from 7pm-1am

Welcome to mixology central, a bar where watching your drink being made is nearly as exquisite as sipping it. Their funky cocktails are meticulously concocted and can include bizarre ingredients, such as truffles, mozzarella or grilled fruits. Designed as a roving train, the bar changes themes every three-month, to showcase diverse eccentric specialties and a whole new set of

Central Station

drinks at each new "train station". Call ahead to book. Drinks go from LBP 15.000/10$ onwards.

#hipsterbartenders #cocktailaddicts #dolladolla

DICTATEUR
30 Badawi St. Mar Mikhael
Telephone: +961 (0)3 251 512
Monday-Friday from 5pm-late;
Saturday-Sunday from noon-late

Drinks here are pretty fucking good and, in an unashamedly hipster way, are served with popcorn. The setting is quite cool too, and ideal for big groups as space is not an issue here.

Recommended drink: cucumber smash (LBP 12.000/8$).

#underground #bignightsout #nomoneynomore

Q INTERNAZIONALE

Armenia St./Alexander Fleming St. Mar Mikhael
Telephone: +961 (0)1 565463
Daily from 7pm-late

Step into this groovy bar and fasten your seat belt as you're in for a night – at least the retro inside-of-an-airplane photograph on the wall suggests so. Apparently named after some football club in Milan (we wouldn't know...), we're glad to say the place is no sports bar! The music here is always funky and the impressive list of cocktail drinks tends to make us smile (around LBP 12.000/8$). If you come more than once, bartenders always seem to remember your last order.

#boozynights #youngfriendlyandtrashed

R VYVYAN'S

Armenia St. Mar Mikhael
Telephone: +961 (0)1 567040
Daily from 10am-3am

This cozy little hole-in-the-wall is an intellectual hangout café during the day and a banging cocktail bar at night. FYI: the owner is known to be obsessed by Oscar Wilde and actually named this bar after the renowned writer's son.

Recommended drink: Gin basil smash (LBP 13.000/8.5$).

#richhipsters #bohemian

BOURJ HAMMOUD & DORA

- **A** Abou Abdallah
- **B** Abou Hassan
- **C** Al Hana
- **D** Onno
- **E** Varouj
- **F** The Wine Teller
- **G** Apo Kebab
- **H** Basterma Bedo
- **I** Basterma Mano

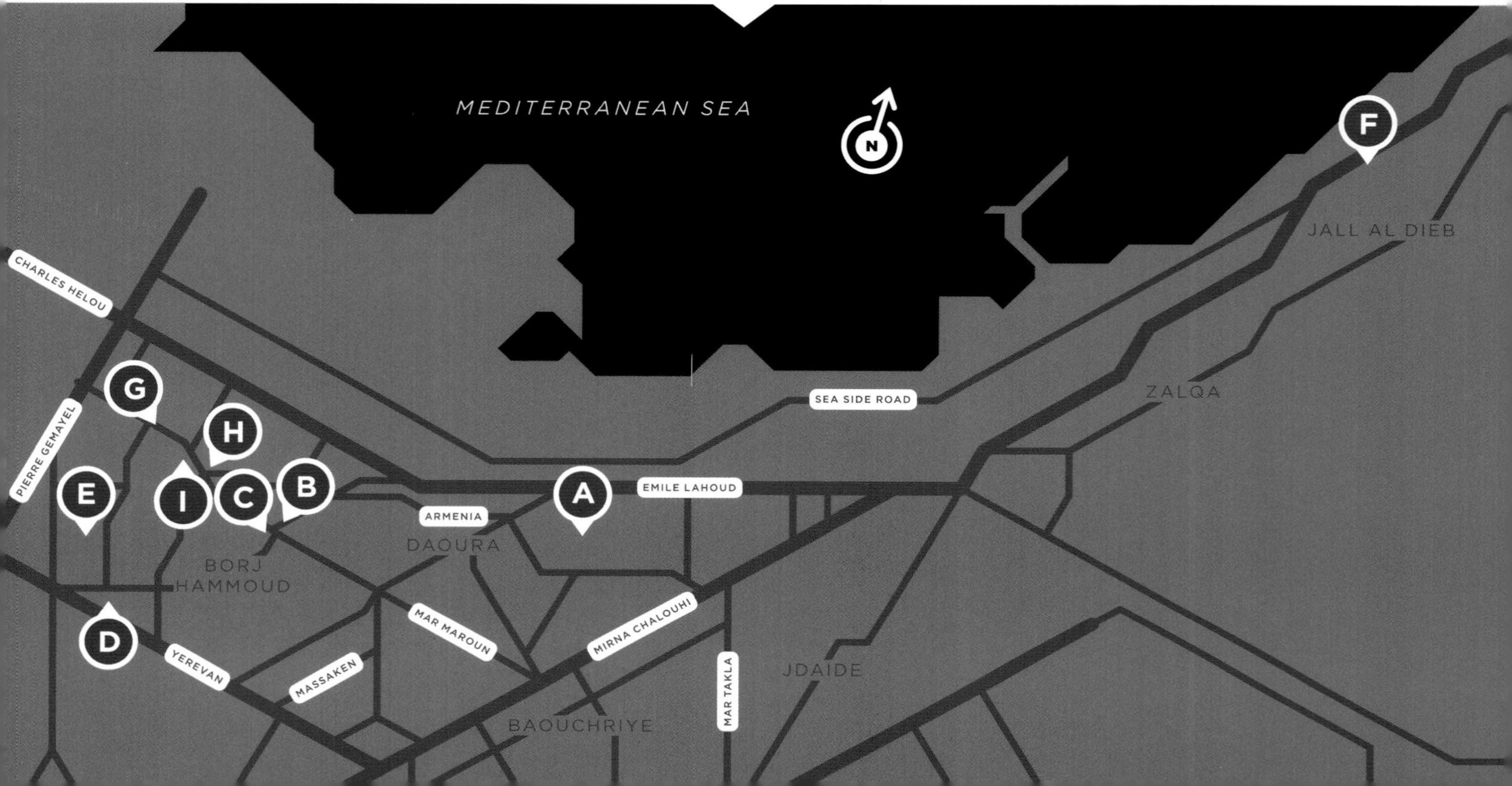

BOURJ HAMMOUD & DORA

Mainly populated by Armenians, this industrious area was founded by survivors of the 1915 incident that cannot be mentioned. Known for its many jewellers, and truly yummy food – Bourj Hammoud has a stinky flaw: its smell. The polluted river running through the neighbourhood is filled with raw sewage and other nasties, so make sure to block your nose before your promenade. Once you've made your way in over the bridge though, sniff the air and follow your grumbling tummy, which will lead you to exquisite places.

Slightly further away is Dora. This residential area is where foreign labourers live or hang out due to the cheap shops and restaurants. It also happens to be where many locals score their drugs, so beware.

RESTAURANTS

A ABOU ABDALLAH
Pierre Gemayel St. Behind Mercedes Company, Dora
Telephone: +96 (0)1 256286
Monday–Saturday from 7am-2pm

Established in 1956 by Youssef el Khoury and his wife, this modest little gem has become quite in demand. All the Mezze here are from family recipes and are absolutely divine. We especially recommend their *Fatteh*; it deserves a medal.

#fattehfever

ⓑ ABOU HASSAN

Haret Sader, Bourj Hammoud
Telephone: +961 (0)1 266880
Daily from 9am-12.30am

This *Fatteh* and *Hummus* sanctuary may not look like much but is so amazingly mouth-watering that customers include politicians, actors, taxi drivers and workers. In short: everybody wants to have a taste.

Orgasmic Hummus with pine nuts

Recommended dish: Hummus with pine nuts (LBP 6.500/4.5$).

#nobooze #buteveryoneiswelcome

C AL HANA
Mar Youssef St. behind Rojican, Bourj Hammoud
Telephone: +961 (0)1 266297
Daily from 9am-12.30am

Right across from Abu Hassan, with its homey Hummus, Foul and Fatteh, Al Hana is pretty much the same deal only prepared the Christian way, as opposed to the Muslim. The menu is only in Arabic, so try to come prepared, or point and wish for the best!

#chickpeasineverydish

Mouth-watering Fatteh

D ONNO

Aghabios St. Bourj Hammoud
Telephone: +961 (0)3 801476
Monday-Saturday from 9.30am-9.30pm

Another superb Armenian eatery situated in the heart of Bourj Hammoud. Walk up the stairs and take a seat. Located below an overhead highway, this place looks a little rustic, but the excellent cuisine makes up for the minimalist décor. Onno cooks up all the usual treats at an affordable price.

#tattoedwaiters

E VAROUJ

Maracha Royal St. Bourj Hammoud
Telephone: +961 (0)3 882933
Monday-Saturday from 12.30pm-4.30pm, 7.30pm-11.30pm

Positioned in a narrow alleyway, this confined Armenian is not the easiest to find but should definitely not be missed. Everything about this place is surreal, from the wooden American-ranch feel with stuffed dead animals and pistols for decoration, to the ill-humoured owner. No menus are provided here, you simply get what the owner feels like giving you. Don't be offended if he says no to some suggestions you may have, as that's just the way he is.

Hopefully, you will be lucky enough to try their scrumptiously rich and creamy *Hummus*, which we still dream about, or their smooth, yet slightly bitter stuffed aubergine with what we guessed was coriander, onions, parsley, chickpeas and pine nuts. We asked, but the owner remained mute.

Varouj's scrumptious Hummus

Warning: the bill is not really a fixed price; it varies depending on the impression you made. But a meal for two with drinks is roughly LBP 75.000/50$.

Recommended dish: the perfectly seasoned juicy frogs legs in garlic, lemon and olive oil.

#youwillprobablygetlost #nomenuisthebestmenu

BARS

F THE WINE TELLER

Jal El Dib Highway, Matar Abou Jaoudeh St., after Dora
Telephone: +961 (0)1 4 722 602
Monday from 11am-7pm;
Tuesday-Saturday from 11am-11pm

This quaint little shop, right on the outskirt of Dora, specializes in all things wine, with a selection of over 200 Lebanese and 250 International ones to choose from. Part-time bar à vin, this establishment combines wine with small portions of food to enhance the palate. Tasting 3 wines ranges from LBP 75.000/50$, with the usual cheese and charcuterie, to LBP 115.000/75$ served with salmon, foie gras or duck magret. We recommend Ourjouan wine, a label created by the owner himself, Mr Moutran, a renowned wine master who also organizes proper wine tasting session at his cellar. Call ahead to inquire.

Recommended drink: Afandello, the Lebanese Limoncello with clementines used instead of the traditional lemon.

#impressyourdate #savewaterdrinkwine

STREET FOOD

ⓖ APO KEBAB
Harboyan Center, Block A, Tiro St. Bourj Hammoud
Telephone: +961 (0)1 261789
Monday-Saturday from 11am-8.30pm; Sunday from 11am-3pm

Unlike the Turkish *Kebab*, the Armenian one doesn't rotate on a skewer. Here the meat is minced (generally half mutton, half lamb), mixed with herbs and spices, baked in a wood-fired oven, served with vegetables in a Lebanese flatbread and seasoned to your taste. Located on a dodgy backstreet, Apo serves out-of-this-world *Kebab*s topped with roasted almonds, fragrant sauces and other yummies.

🐦 #10typesofkebabs

ⓗ BASTERMA BEDO
Municipality Park, Bourj Hammoud
Telephone: +961 (0)1 261 439
Daily from 7am-10pm

Have you had the chance to taste this salty cured Armenian beef called *Basterma*? If you dig it, then head over to this *Basterma* retreat for a fine-looking selection. (Sandwich LBP 4.000/2.5$).

🐦 #armeniangoodies

Basterma

① BASTERMA MANO

Blanco Center, Municipality St. Bourj Hammoud
Telephone: +961 (0)1 268560
Daily from noon-late

Hungry for some cured meat? This deli prepares some juicy sandwiches on the go, and sells meat by the kilo. The Basterma *Shawarma* is ideal on your way back from a big night out. The onions are quite heavy on the breath though, so try to go solo or with good friends.

🐦 #stinkybreath #meatlovers # joeytribbiani

TAHINOV HATS (IN ARMENIAN) OR TAHINOV WITH SUGAR

These sweet sesame paste wraps are fucking good and can be found all around Bourj Hammoud. Whether for breakfast, dessert or as a sweet-treat, everything goes, but just be careful, as the amount of calories in each is gargantuan.

Bourj Hammoud is known for selling some flavoursome spices

• SIN EL FIL •

A Marky's **B** Le Phenicien

SIN EL FIL

Sin El Fil, which for no apparent reason literally translates as the elephant's tooth, is a north-eastern suburb of Beirut. The mainly residential area contains many shopping malls, businesses, hospitals and fortunately for us, a few restaurants.

STREET FOOD

A MARKY'S

Horch Tabet Main Road Before Mkaless Roundabout, Sin El Fil
Telephone: +961 (0)1 511801
Daily from noon-12am Delivery service available

This Beiruti fast-food chain is the country's first real Philly joint, known for its tenderly juicy burgers. From the Le Canadien philly steak sandwich with grilled onions, poutine gravy and homemade cheese curds (LBP 10.500/7$) to the Go West Burger made of 5oz beef patty, mayo, BBQ sauce, grilled onions, bacon, and American cheese (LBP 11.000/7.30$), their stuff is tight. Their fries though, not so much.

#nobodysperfect

One of Marky's delicious burgers

RESTAURANTS

🅱 LE PHENICIEN

Sfeir Bldg, Dimitri el Hayek St. Horch Tabet, Sin El Fil
Telephone: +961 (0)1 499177
Daily from 12.30pm-3.15pm, 8.15pm-11pm

Opened after the original Tyr restaurant, many consider dishes here to be golden. Decorated like the interior of a ship, this tasty fish restaurant is especially loved by older people who seem to know what they're talking about. Their specialty is their Sayadiyeh, but their whole menu is a treat.

🐦 #fishisking #prawnisqueen

Fresh prawns from Le Phenicien

Lockstock is a great spot for after work drinks

NEW SPOTS

Watch out for these newly opened spots!

BEYT
Geara building, Armenia St. Mar Mikhael
Telephone: +961 (0)1 444110
Monday–Saturday from 11am-8.30pm for tea and homemade cakes, and once every 2 weeks for dinner

This charming newly opened Bed & Breakfast is taking 40 diners to a different culinary destination every couple of weeks. Think Sri Lanka, Thailand or Ethiopia. Check out their Facebook page (www.facebook.com/PlanBEY) to find out about their next exciting buffet. (LBP 30.000/20$/p)

LOCK STOCK
Armenia St. right next to Vyvyan's (p.149), Mar Mikhael
Telephone: +961 76 773 277
Daily from 10am-3am

By the same peeps behind Julep's (p.82), this bar is bound to be a success. Bartenders here insist in guessing what drink to make you – and, in our experience, they're spot on. The décor also happens to be excruciatingly cute, in a NY West Village kinda way.

MARIO E MARIO

39 Patriarche St. Mar Mikhael
Telephone: +961 (0)1 444036
Monday-Sunday from 7.30pm-12am

A project in the making for many years (we would know, the owner – Mario Haddad – first told us about it during an interview over two years ago), this cute eatery is finally ready. Its concept: home cooked Italian cuisine in a charming house that feels like home. The menu is fresh and changes daily (do expect to splurge though, as this is the same dude behind Sushi Bar p.110) Best part? The free Limoncello shots at the end of your meal.

DAWAWINE

Akkar Building, 2nd Floor, Arz St. Gemmayzeh
Telephone: +961 (0)1 567705
Tuesday – Sunday from 11am- 11pm

This Library meets cultural center meets café/restaurant is the perfect quiet spot to get some work done. The affordable French menu is presented on a black board and includes fresh salads (salmon and orange green salad LBP 16.000/11$), funky sandwiches (brie and red berry jam baguette LBP 9.000/6$) and tasty platters.

A colourful salmon and orange green salad at Dawawine

OUTSIDE OF BEIRUT

- Bekaa
  - **A** Chtaura
  - **B** Zahlé
  - **C** Anjar

- Mount Lebanon
  - **D** Jounieh
  - **E** Jbeil or Byblos
  - **F** Batroun

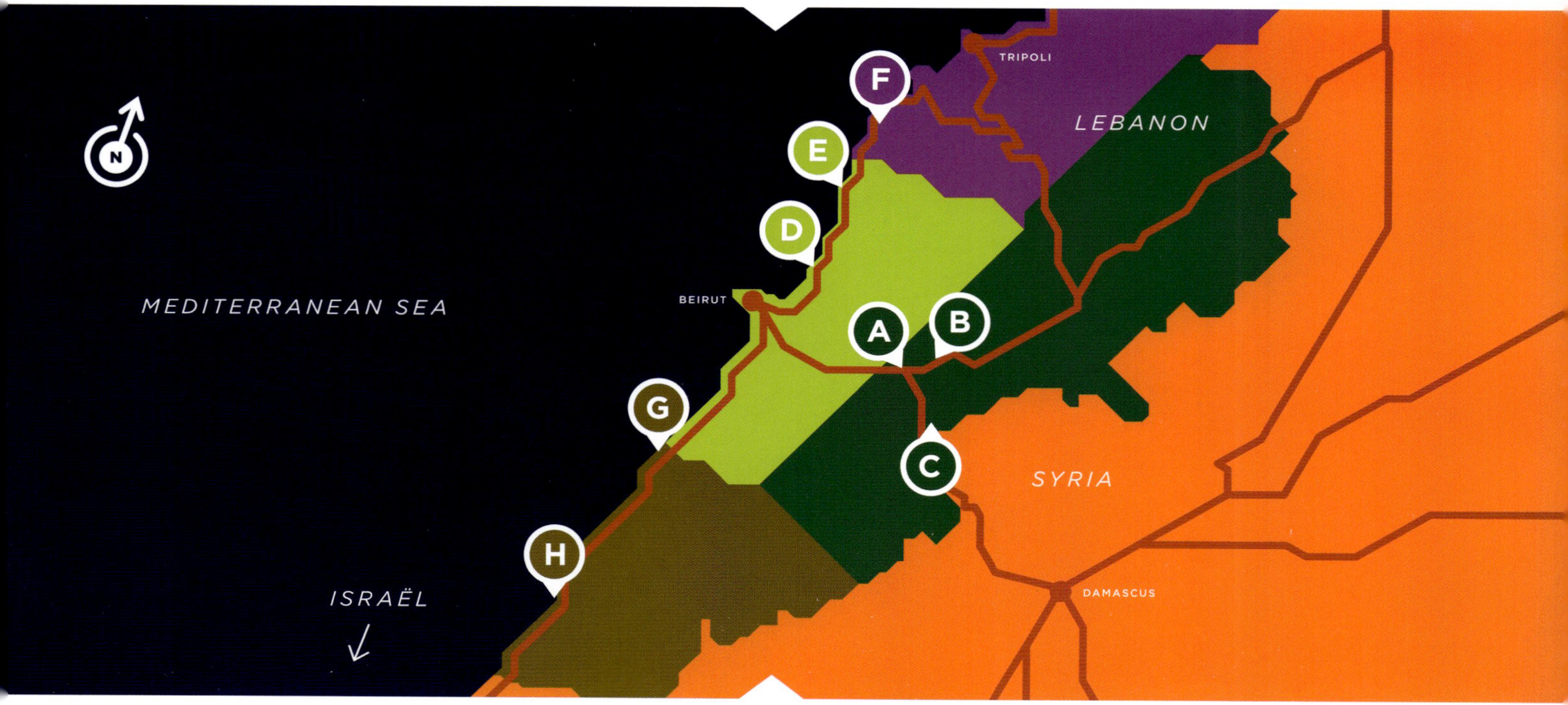

- North Lebanon

- South Lebanon
  - **G** Sidon
  - **H** Sour or Tyre

OUTSIDE BEIRUT: THE BEKAA VALLEY

This fertile and extraordinarily beautiful valley is located between Mount Lebanon, the Anti-Lebanon Mountains and Syria. The gorge holds the country's biggest vineyards and an abundant number of fruits and vegetables. Unfortunately, due to the recent conflicts in Syria, areas of the Bekaa that are very close to the warring country have suffered, which means many culinary institutions have shut down due to clashes or lack of clientele.

A CHTAURA AND BEYOND

The city of Chtaura is located on the way to the Bekaa and, to our biggest delight, is filled with milk, cheeses, and all our beloved dairy products, notably *Darfiyeh*, *Labneh*, *Areesh*, *Jibne* – to name but a few. Lactose intolerants: keep out!

SHOPS

JABER JABER & SONS
Mreyjat, main road, Chtaura
Telephone: +961 (0)8 544836
Daily from 7am-10pm

Cheese lovers, this one is for you! Whether you are strolling through Beirut or going up to the Bekaa, you simply must stop by Jaber Jaber & Sons. Since 1928, this father to son (hence the name) grocery shop only sells fresh produce from the region with no additives or any other nasties. They focus on dairy products, such as soft cheeses and milk but you can also find other tasty ingredients like eggs, honey and jam.

Their speciality is the *Areesh* sandwich (fresh soft cheese that is basically fermented milk sprinkled with honey and served in a wrap); a flawless breakfast or snack that will leave you wanting more.

LAITERIE DU COUVENT DE TAANAYEL

Main road, Taanayel
Telephone: +961 (0)8 543101

Early birds: come watch cows get milked; lazy-asses: rent a bike for that dearly needed exercise, and explore this milk farm. And everyone: try to get your hands on their specialty, Lebanese Gouda, which oddly resembles Parmesan.

#thesimplelife

LAITERIE HADWANE

Main road, Mreijat
Telephone: +961 (0)8 540625
Daily from 8am-6pm

As the Bekaa's most popular and renowned cheese-shop, you may just have to get in line. From tasty cheeses sold by the kilogram to incredible *Labneh* sandwiches to eat on the go, when the Hadwane family's involved - you're good to go!

#cantgetenoughcheese

RESTAURANTS

TAWLET AMMIQ

Ammiq, West Bekaa
Telephone: +961 (0)3 004481
Tuesday-Friday from 9am-4pm à la carte service; Saturday-Sunday from 1pm-4pm buffet.

Closed during winter season. Being a personal favourite of ours, we were certain no place in the country could beat Beirut's Tawlet restaurant – and we were wrong. The eco-restaurant's second branch and possible better half may only be open during the sunnier months, but is worth the detour. With the buffet combo carefully prepared using local farmers' produce, it's pretty much the same deal as in Beirut, only better and with a breath-taking view of the Bekaa valley included in the banqueting-experience. A la carte dishes from LBP 22.500/15$. Buffet is LBP 60.000/40$.

#weekendbuffet #360degreepanorama #lovefallingsetting

VISIT & TASTE

MASSAYA
Main road, Taanayel
Telephone: +961 (0)8 510 135
Summer: Monday-Saturday from 8am-4.30pm; Sunday from 10am-5.30pm Winter: Monday-Friday from 8am-4pm; Saturday from 9am-noon Open on Sunday (except storms)

The Ghosn brothers initially only produced Arak but very soon collaborated with some big French wine producers and began making their own. Described by the New York Times as Lebanon's "hippest" wine, we must add that even their *Arak* is quite a treat.

#wineorarak? #getboth

🅑 ZAHLÉ AND BEYOND

Located 1,000m up the mountains and 52km away from buzzing Beirut, Zahlé is an ideal escape from the capital, even though it remains one of the largest towns in Lebanon. The subject of many songs and sonnets, the town of Zahlé welcomes visitors with a statue of a woman covered in grapes, to remind all that it is the city of poetry and wine.

--- SHOPS ---

NIDAL RAYESS
1st floor, Bakar & Chatila building
Damascus International road Jdita

This little boutique produces *Labneh, Halloumi* and everything dairy. Come watch them get down to business and make the cheeses from scratch. Under no circumstance should you forget to taste their apricot jam though, as it is truly delicious.

--- RESTAURANTS ---

CASINO MHANNA
Berdawni - by the river, Zahlé

If you've got time to enjoy the scenery and take a seat, head over to the dainty Bardouni river, surrounded by buzzing restaurants. Mhanna, which has a few branches open around the country, serves good Mezze but at a high price. Meal for two LBP 60.000/50$.

🐦 #alotoffruitfordessert

SNACKS

ADEL MASSAAD
Mar Elias neighborhood
Telephone: +961 (0)8 807677

In a hurry, or simply passing by? Grab one (or two) of Adel Massaad's tasty super-slim anorexic looking sandwiches.

WALID KHALAF
Telephone: +961 (0)3 408880

Craving something refreshingly sweet? If so, there's no better stop to hop to than Khalf & Abou Sleiman's ice cream joint for some traditional *kashta* (boiled milk mixed with crushed ice and spices).

🐦 #iceicebaby

VISIT & TASTE

We don't know about you, but for us after lunch seems like an appropriate time to get drinking, and since you happen to be at the ideal spot for both wine and Arak tastings, why not head over to either:

CHATEAU KSARA
Zahle main road
Telephone: +961 (0)8 813495

Legend has it that a fox chasing hens discovered the most ancient natural caves of the land, at the ideal wine preservation temperature of 12°C, in 1898. This winery's success has been quite significant ever since.

🐦 #freeguidedtour

CHATEAU KHOURY
Zahle, Dhour Zahle
Telephone: +961 (0)8 801160

Pink grapes were planted here resulting in some delicious Pinot Grigio and Riesling.

🐦 #wedrinkanycolor #antiracism

(C) ANJAR & BEYOND

A quiet destination known for its rich Armenian cultural influences, it was a safe- zone for refugees who escaped Turkey in 1915. 30 years later, archeologists discovered the layout of a walled Roman town, said to date from the first century of Islam, which got Anjar listed as a UNESCO World Heritage site. Although the 1300 year-old city is primarily known for its trout, don't let that stop you from digging into a couple of other things.

RESTAURANT

SHAMS
Entrance of the city, Anjar
Telephone: +961 (0)8 620567
Daily from noon-10pm

The city's yummiest restaurant, Shams, offers all the usual Lebanese suspects. If you really want to be tastebuddingly impressed though, get some of their patented potato balloons.

#goodandcheap

SNACK

FURN KOCH ANJAR
Koch St. Anjar
Daily from 8am-2pm

Get your ass to this old-school Armenian bakery, and order a *Shanklich* (fermented cheese) *Manouche*!

#traditionalcooking

VISIT & TASTE

CHATEAU KEFRAYA
Kefraya village
Telephone: +961 (0)8 645333

A 40-minute drive southwest of Anjar, this place is worth the detour. If not to see 400 wine-filled hectares, producing over 2 million bottles a year, then at least to drink it!

#somethingabitmoreelaborate

Al Sultan Brahim's stunning view on the coastline

MOUNT LEBANON

Ranging from the sea to the mountains, Mount Lebanon offers quite a variety of products, including fish and game. The diversity of this region is so vast that one can go from dining at the beach, feet deep in the sea, to eating fondue and skiing away in just a couple of hours.

D JOUNIEH & BEYOND

Known as Beirut's suburb, Jounieh isn't exactly pretty. The buildings are tall, the traffic flows fast and the air is polluted. The restaurants aren't lacking though, and are really quite impressive. If/when you decide to visit this part of town, whether it's on your way up north or to get out of the city, try to avoid the traffic! (Dodge mornings and afternoons during the week, and 12-2pm and 6-7pm on the weekend)!

--- **RESTAURANTS** ---

ABOU WALID
Bouar main road, Jounieh
Telephone: +961 (0)3 908381

A cheap alternative to a ravishing banquet, this is where you'll find the middle classes who laugh at those who spend hundreds on fish.

The funny thing is that Lebanon's richest don't even know this little jewel exists.

🐦 #eatmoreforless

AL SULTAN BRAHIM
Near Casino, Sea Side Rd, Jounieh
Telephone: +961 (0)9 853753
Daily from noon-12am

Same deal as the one in downtown Beirut, only with a beautiful view of the sea and a funky architectural setting.

🐦 #bringyouryacht

Diners enjoying Al Sultan Brahim's delectable Mezze by the shore

BABEL
Dbayeh high way
Telephone: +961 70425777
Daily from noon-12am

Sumptuous traditional dishes with a slight twist are served here, in a huge space, at an unfortunately high price. This restaurant actually has a VIP section (lol) and is considered by many to be one of the best Lebanese eateries in town.

#dinneratacastle #costmillionstobuilt

CHEZ SAMI
Maameltein, Jounieh Old Rd
Telephone: +961 (0)9 910520
Daily from noon-12am

Many say this is the best of the many fresh fish restaurants found in Lebanon. Located on the outskirt of Beirut, with (again) a view on the sea and the city, you'll find yourself licking your fingers.

#foodorgasm #dolladolla

HABANA
Sarba, Jounieh
Telephone: +961 (0)9 638166
Daily from 7.30pm- 1.30am

Habana is all about tasty Mexican cuisine in a colonial house with tequila and cocktails that will quickly get you perky.

#AyPapi

LE GALET
Tabarja Old Road, Facing the municipality, Jounieh
Telephone: +961 (0)9 853872

Fresh seafood served in a cosy setting.

#funkyaquarium

TABLE FINE
Jounieh Souks
Telephone: +961 (0)9 919666
Tuesday-Sunday from 12.30pm-3pm, 8.30pm-11pm

As one of the few (maybe even only) restaurants in Lebanon with a three-times Michelin starred chef, Jerome Serres. Table Fine serves haute Mediterranean cuisine, with innovative dishes, such as lobster guacamole, all while providing its clientele with a lovely view.

#superstar

SNACK

ABOU ANDRE
Makhlouf Building, Maameltein, Jounieh Main Road
Telephone: +961 (0)3 345010

With their mouthwatering *Hummus*, eggs with *Awarma*, *Fatteh* and *Falafel*, we strongly urge you to try this place.

FOOD ACTIVITY

DBAYE FISHING CLUB

La Marina Joseph Khoury, Sea Side Rd, Dbayeh
Telephone: +961 (0)3 256626
www.dbayefishingclub.com

Dbaye offers fishing lessons for all levels out on their fully equipped boats – providing the weather is right, so do call ahead to inquire. "You can't have your cake and eat it" doesn't apply here, as you get to take your catch home and do whatever you please with it.

#sittingonthedockofthebay

THE SHOUF & BEYOND

The Shouf is Lebanon's greenest region. It has a stunning nature reserve, and "akoub" (an edible asparagus-meets-artichoke vegetable), sweet figs, pomegranates and carobs all grow here. Another local specialty, also common in South America, is the "mate" (a tea-like drink made of dried yerba mate leaves), which locals drink daily. The hot beverage was born in Paraguay but spread through the South American continent with the help of missionaries and was later brought to Lebanon, at the end of the XIXth century, by Druze expatriates.

--- SHOPS ---

NABEEL EL AYYAS
Barouk
Telephone: +961 (0)3 438723

After a long hike uphill, it's clearly time for a little treat. Give this spot a visit to witness the making of some sweet cedar honey. The bees produce several hundred kilos of cedar honey per year, and Nabeel sells the sweet stuff to visitors and hikers.

SHOUF BIOSPHERE RESERVE
Maaser el chouf, Village square, facing public garden entrance
Telephone: +961 (0)5 350250
Daily from 9am-5pm

Souvenir hunters: three wonderful boutiques filled with local produce hide within this nature reserve. We're talking forested honeys, wild pine thyme and flavoursome jams!

#hiking #biking #donkeyriding #snowshoeing #eating

RESTAURANTS

AKRAM MAHMOUD GUESTHOUSE

Taameer St. Barouk
Telephone: +961 (0)3 829102
(Have to be 6-8 people, and reserve 48hours in advance)

The hostess of this warm guesthouse is a cordon bleu, and enjoys preparing her home-cooked meals made with vegetables from her garden, for all her guests to delight in.

#perfectafterahike

FAKHREDDINE

Baakline - village road
Telephone: +961 (0)5 300821
Daily from 8am-10pm (closed on Wednesday and Thursday)

Service may be a tad slow here, as the couple that owns the place have quite a few years behind them. If you're in no rush though, their unique Foul and their own version of broad beans seasoned with a lemon-cumin sauce are meticulously prepared with love, and definitely worth the wait.

HALIM
Mahatta St. Bhamdoun Main Road
Telephone: +961 (0)5 260030

Opened since 1924, this little gem has survived it all. "Don't judge a book by its cover" should be their slogan as the decoration is pretty ugly, but the food is where it's at. Apologies to vegetarians, as this

Half a dozen pomegranate "assafir" birds at Halim

place might repulse you. Known for its delicious locally hunted "assafir", you will just have to be prepared to chew some crunchy bones, as the charcoal-grilled little birds are not decorticated. The sparrows are served in their juicy fat and are generally eaten rolled in *Markouk* bread and dipped in *Sumac* spice, to add a little sour taste. Different preparations are also available to complement the birdies; try the sweet and sour lemon aroma, or the thick and rich pomegranate flavour. To accompany the feast, we strongly recommend their locally distilled *Arak* baladi, which is refreshingly light yet rather effective. All in all, Halim is a great pit stop on your way up to the Bekaa!

#peoplewhodontmindsittingonplasticchairs #byebyebirdie

DRINKS

THE MATÉ FACTORY
Aley, main road
Telephone: +961 (0)5 556123
Daily from 9am-5pm

Not the cosiest of hangouts but good enough to indulge in maté-based tea, coffee and pastries.

🐦 #notfromlebanon #immunebooster

SNACKS

WARD
Bhamdoun, Main road, in the old town
Telephone: +961 (0)3 224032
Daily from 8am-6pm

One word: *Tamriyeh*. This little bakery makes some of the country's tastiest Arabic sweets with ground semolina, orange blossom water and sugar. Although the damaging pastry is fried in oil and concealed in powdered sugar, these 5 seconds of pleasure may just be worth it.

VISIT & TASTE

CHATEAU MUSAR
Kfour, near Dlebta
Telephone: +961 (0)1 201828
Call ahead

Funnily enough, when there's wine, the French always seem to be involved. The vines of this chateau were planted in the '30s, as French soldiers stationed in the area craved their happy juice. With red, white and even some Arak to choose from: happiness will quickly make its way to you too!

#atwaitrosefor£18

KESERWAN & BEYOND

There's no lack of Lebanese gastronomy in this high-altitude district. The air is purer, the sky is clearer and the food itself seems to be tastier. Time to get climbing – and eating!

SHOP

YAZBECK HONEY
General Khalil Kanaan St. Jdeidet
Telephone: +961 (0)1 890 644
Daily from 9am-4pm closed on Sunday

If you've felt inspired by all the marvellous honey in Lebanon and want to create your own, head down to this store where all the honey-making essentials are sold – beehive included!

#everyoneshouldownahoneykit

RESTAURANTS

AL HALABI
Antelias Square, next to St. Elie Center, Antelias
Telephone: +961 (0)4 523555
Daily from noon-11pm

One of the country's oldest restaurants, Al Halabi, consistently delivers delicious authentic dishes and great service. From their amazing Hummus and their Moudardara to their Mouhalabieh, your palate will thank you.

#somethingsneverchange

BOTTEGA
Mhaydseh Bridge, Bikfaya, Metn
Telephone: +961 (0)4 984555

Need a change from Arabic food? This intimate and modest Italian restaurant surprisingly prepares some pretty damn good food. Garlic bread LBP 7.000/5$.

#salmonpizza

CHEZ MOUNIR
Broumana, Camille Bld, Chamoun
Telephone: +961 (0)4 873900
Daily from noon-11pm

Chez Mounir has so much more to offer than its enchanting garden-esque setting. The traditional cuisine is as divine as the service is immaculate. No comment.

#nohashtag

FADEL
Naas Village. Bikfaya
Telephone: +961 (0)4 980979
Daily from 12.30pm-4.30pm, 7.30pm-12.30am

Sunday family lunches are sacred in this country, but not as revered as getting a reservation on that holy day at Fadel. This renowned restaurant, located up in the mountains, serves some of the country's best food. Their set Mezze menu comes in huge portions with all the usual suspects – but better. Their *Bayd w Awarma* (eggs and fatty meat) or *Hummus Awarma* (same fatty meat) are exquisite. Make sure to skip your previous meal: you'll need the stomach space.

#sundaylunch #dipkibbehinhummus #ogres

LE MONTAGNOU
Ayoun el Semane, Faraya
Telephone: +961 (0)3 341441
Daily from noon-12am

Being the Courchevel of Lebanon, the Faraya Mountains are very hip, however they do leave a little to be desired slope-wise. With its mind-blowing view and cozy wooden interior, Montagnou is the Alp's favourite food-stop and is ideal to warm yourself up over a jolly and creamy fondue savoyarde, (LBP 98.000/65$ for two) or a tasty pierrade de viande (LBP 95.000/64$ for two). No need to wait for winter to stopover, the summer view is just as exceptional.

#hiournameisdontbelieveinjetlagandweareaddictedtocheese

SNACKS

LE GOURMET
Metn, Bikfaya
Telephone: +961 (0)4 980876

This joint has been selling tasty chicken baguette-sandwiches with pickles and homemade garlic paste since 1976. Sahtein!

MAR CHARBEL BAKERY
By the Hrajel Roundabout

Charming Afif will welcome you with his lovely smile to taste his succulent *Lahmacun* (baked thin bread topped with minced meat, vegetables and herbs, seasoned with lemon). Beware: the shop may be gross, but the wrap is truly delicious.

SINIOUR

Main road, Antelias
Telephone: +961 (0)4 419970
Daily from 8am-12am

The tastiest *Manouche* of the region is freshly baked here.

VISIT & TASTE

961 BEER

Mazraat Yachouh - Industrial zone
Telephone: +961 (0)3 222331

Who would've thought that a hipster beer could come out of such an ancient land? Founded during the 2006 war, 961 Beer – named after the country's area code – it went from a 20-litre kettle production to 2 million litres brewed last year. Beers include American Amber Lager, Red Ale, English Brown Porter, Belgian Witbier and Lebanese pale ale – and frankly all should be sampled. For events, tastings and tours check out their Facebook page or give them a call. For guidance on "How to taste Beer" and tips on preparing food, their webpage (www.961.com) is where it's at.

#downit

E JBEIL & AMSHEET

Jbeil (also named Byblos) is a charming Phoenician city, which is said to have been built by Kronos, the leader of the first generation of Titans. The town is particularly interesting for archaeologists and architecture-enthusiasts, as Neolithic remains can be spotted, with some still to be found. Its culinary specialty is definitely fish, and hungry visitors come to admire the old souk, the fortress, the charismatic harbour and its yearly summer music festival.

SHOP

ADONIS VALLEY
Fatri - main road
Telephone: +961 (0)3 456336
Daily from 10am-4pm

A growing boutique that sells organic yummies, from grape molasses spread, and apple vinegar to sun-dried tomatoes.

EDDÉS HERBS
Old souk, Jbeil
Telephone: +961 (0)9 54 22 26
Daily from 9am-8pm

Looking for something different to take back home? Pierrot sells a wide selection of local plants, roots and herbs to spice up your home-cooked meals.

FLEUR DE LAIT
Main road Fatri
Telephone: +961 (0)9 420709
Daily from 9am-8pm

An artisans dairy-shop... ideal to taste, enjoy and acquire!

RESTAURANTS

CHEZ ZAKHIA
Amchit Port
Telephone: +961 (0)9 621717
Daily from 12.30pm-12am

Enjoy delicious fish while appreciating the gorgeous view of the sea and watching other fish play. This is a great romantic spot to take your plus one or even a wannabe plus one.

#wefoundnemo

ÉCAFÉ
Edde Yark, Old Souk, Byblos
Telephone: +961 (0)9 54 22 24
Daily from 8am-12am

This French/Italian courtyard restaurant, known for its outdoor grill, is surrounded by the souk's honey-coloured stonewalls. The "café" emphasizes on fresh ingredients and juicy cuts of meat. Get yourself some tasty frozen lemonade to help you gulp down your ferocious feast. On Sundays, George's piano tunes will jazz up your brunch and on Wednesday nights, come along for some wine and fromage.

🐦 #isthisparis?

LOCANDA A LA GRANDA
Old Souk, Pepe Abed St. Facing Castle Main Gate, Jbeil
Telephone: +961 (0)9 944 333
Daily from noon-11pm

Funky dishes with a slight fusion twist are offered at this Lebanese restaurant. The setting is grandiose with a stunning view of the historic old port of Byblos. Bring your special someone, indulge in their chicken *Osmalliyeh* and hopefully you'll get lucky.

MOTHER
Old town, Unesco square, Byblos
Telephone: +961 (0) 03 951 901
Daily from noon-12am

This miniature French restaurant serves oven roasted melted Camembert to our cheese-loving ass' delight.

🐦 #nomorecellulite

PEPE'S FISHING CLUB

Pepe Abed, Old Souk, Byblos
Telephone: +961 (0)3 635850
Daily from 10am-12am

We understand Brigitte Bardot used to come here during Lebanon's golden age – but then again we probably should admit to you that we're a tad gullible. Either way, Pepe serves some good fish and Mezze by the charming harbour.

#theyshoweduspictures

SNACK

FURN EL SABAYA

Amchit Sea Road,
Telephone: +961 (0)9 624 466
Daily from 7am-2pm

Owned by the four Zughaib sisters, this famous bakery was specifically opened to provide traditional baked delicacies which were no longer available in larger retail stores. Although the *Furn* produces both sweet and savoury pastries, such as *Manouche* and *Lahm bi ajeen*, the siblings are well known for their *Mouwaraka* (from LBP 5.000/3.5$), using a recipe their mother passed on to them. Their jewel consists of sweet dough aromatized in both rose and orange blossom water and with a walnut and almond filling (yum, right?).

#sisterscanworktogether #privatejoke

Eat with your feet in the water at Jammal (see p.200)

THE NORTH

Its name might sound quite scary, in a Game of Thrones "winter's coming" kinda' way, but this couldn't be further from the truth. Contrary to what its label might imply, the north holds many beautiful beaches and stunning landscapes. Its capital city, Tripoli, was known for its succulent specialties and delicacies but has sadly suffered tremendously from the neighbouring Syrian Civil war and is no longer safe to visit.

The area conceals many little treasures and beauties though!

ⓕ BATROUN

This cute coastal town offers charismatic rock beaches, a Phoenician wall and a range of endearing restaurants.

RESTAURANTS

BATROUNIYAT
Main road Batroun
Telephone: +961 (0)6 744510
Monday-Friday from noon-10pm; open Sunday buffet

This refurbished old beautiful mansion serves luscious local cuisine with constantly fluctuating regional specialties. Try to keep some of your appetite for dessert, as their pastries usually come from the famous Hallab bakery in Tripoli.

Tip: visit their Mouneh shop after your meal and get your hands on some of their local foie gras, fresh *Za'atar* or savoury myrtle jam.

BEIT AL BATROUN
Thoum, After Army Checkpoint Batroun
Telephone: +961 (0)3 270049
April to the end of October

This boho-chic bed & breakfast happens to have a marvellous cook as a host (and we've actually featured a couple of her funkiest recipes at the end of this guide). It would be hard for anyone not to have a soft spot for this little baby but go ahead and try it for yourself.

JAMMAL
Kfarabida, just south of Batroun
Telephone: +961 (0)6 740095
Monday-Friday from 11am-6pm; Saturday-Sunday from 11am-11.30pm (late opening on summer weekends only).

Nothing screams paradise like a fresh lunch on a beach, with your toes in the sea and Cuban tunes in the background – but this might turn to hell when you see the bill. As with most coastal eateries, fish is the main deal. Jammal's is particularly delectable and the waiters, dressed in cute sailor outfits, run around making sure you try it. They also encourage you to drink like one, but that's

Sea Bream sashimi

another story. Any fish, cooked any way, with any side you want: easy peasy. The shrimp spring rolls are a nice way to start your meal. For dessert, we insist you try their *Tamriyeh*, as well as their perfectly ripe watermelon.

#richhippies

JOINING
Batroun sea road, right before Jammal
Daily from 12pm-12am

Are you sick and tired of paying a fortune for fish? This little shack prepares theirs beautifully at a good price, and serves it right by the sea on a rocky outcrop. From garlic shrimp and luscious Hummus (seriously), to tender malifa, their dishes are sublime and you'll end up only paying around 25$/head for a feast.

#localhangout #noblingbling

SNACK

FURN MESHAK

Interior road, near Fares Jammal
Telephone: +961 (0)6 740050
Tuesday-Thursday from 4am-2pm Friday-Monday from 2am-2pm

Freshly baked and tailor-made *Manouche*, which will literally make you go "mmm" and pull an orgasmic face as soon as you have a bite.

DRINK

LIMONADE TONY DAOU

Main road, Batroun
Telephone: +961 (0)6 741564

The preciously secret father-to-son lemonade served here is one of the best we've ever tasted. All we know is that lemons are pressed against one another, as opposed to squeezed, and that orange blossom water, sugar and fresh water definitely play a role.

#tryaddingvodka

VISIT & TASTE

IXSIR
Batroun – Basbina
Telephone: +961 71 631 613
Visits schedule: Tuesday, Thursday, Friday, Saturday and Sunday from 9am-4pm Wednesday from 9am-1pm Monday closed. Call to book

Founded by Carlos Ghosn, this wine's name comes from the Arabic "Al-iksir", which literally translates to elixir. Although the group is based in Batroun, their vineyards are spread throughout the country and the vines are respectfully cultivated in a sustainable way.

#greenwine

Relaxed dining at Joining (see p.201)

THE CEDARS

Located 2,500m up in the mountains, this region is named after its 400 odd surviving cedar trees, (one of which you've probably already spotted on the country's flag). During warmer days, Beirutis head here for the much-needed breeze, and in the winter to ski.

RESTAURANTS

SABA
Blaouza main road, leading to Qoszhaya
Telephone: +961 (0)6 645071
Daily from noon-10pm (only weekends during winter)

Serving excellent Shanklich fermented cheese pastries, seamless *Tabouleh* (the specialty of this region) and juicy *Mansaf* chicken, Saba has done a great job of satisfying cravings. Proud diners, who you'll find smiling away, will admit that they've been coming here for over 20 years. Respect.

#loyalty

ZEITOUNI
Main road, Qadisha
Telephone: +961 (0)6 671398
Daily from noon-10pm

The spectacular view, the tasty raw goat's meat and the reasonable prices are always quite tempting here.

#casuallyeatingagoat

Juicy watermelon and sweet
Tamriyeh at Jammal
(see p.200)

THE SOUTH

The South of Lebanon, with its coastline and sunshine, is enchanting to the eye – yet sadly not so much to the taste buds. Unfortunately, due to the Israeli occupation, restaurants and cafes took a serious hit in this region from 1982 onwards and many legendary places closed down. Nowadays, the region offers great products in more of a street grub kinda' way, rather than the usual sit-down restaurant experience. Hop along for the ride if you're an on-the-go type of traveller!

G SAIDA OR SIDON

The city of Saida, which coincides with the modern Arabic word for fishery, used to be a small fishing town at the beginning of the 1900's, but has seen a large growth since. Fishing remains very active today, with catches of the day being sold at the harbour in the early hours through a bidding system.

The charming Old City of Saida resembles an arched maze filled with shops and bakeries, and is known for its yummy sweet treats, like *Chaabiyat*!

SNACKS

ABOU RAMI FALAFEL
Corniche across from the Castle of Saida

Inexplicably delicious *Falafels*, well known throughout the country, which also happen to be super cheap! Add some hot sauce for a lusciously spicy result and if you're a really crazy motherfucker, go all out with pickled chilli peppers.

 #holyfuck

AL ANWAR
Abo Zeid Building, Sitt Nafeeseh St.
Telephone: +961 (0)7 725758
Daily from 8am-7pm, closed on Friday

This old-school and legendary purveyor of Oriental sweets is famous for its real 1001 nights experience; we're talking *Loukoums*, rose water, almond crusts and the classics. Another plus: the salesmen happen to be just as sweet as what they're selling.

 #toocheesy?

AL-JARDALI
Siit Nafeeseh round-about
Telephone: +961 7 729805
Saturday-Thursday from 6am-6pm, Friday from 6am-12pm

Described by locals as making the best Chaabiyat in town, this place tends to be packed. Stand in line and sniff the exquisite air while you listen to the sound of your stomach rumbling – patience is a virtue.

🐦 #waityourturn

FALAFEL AKKAWI
Safa Bldg. Almofti St. Saida
Telephone: +961 (0)7 737114
Daily from 10am-10pm

This father-to-son spot makes great crusty wraps.

🐦 #Ramisgotsomecompetition

"THE ZAHRANI ROAD"

On the road between Saida and Sour, the 24/7 zahrani may look like a crazy slum but is both a meat haven and heaven. Its exquisite BBQ smoke scent can be smelled floating in the air from miles away. Here you can find the whole range from the very best butchers to the ones to avoid. If you unearth a good one, you'll quite literally eat the best *Kebab, Lahm bi ajeen* and raw meat of your life. It's probably best to come with a recommendation though.

🐦 #sorryyoureonyourown #yourturntogiveustips

ⒽSOUR OR TYR

This city translates as "rock" and was originally named after the rocky formation on which it was built. Concealing quite a few gastronomic jewels, this gem clearly stands out in the region.
Its specialties include chicken *Freekeh* and *Frakeh* (raw meat mixed with Burghul and herbs), which are both yum².

RESTAURANTS

BAROUD
Old Souk, Tyr
Telephone: +961 (0)3 949652
Daily from 5am-11am

Come for breakfast to enjoy some divine Foul, Hummus and Msabbaha. It may not look like much from the outside, but the low prices and the gorgeous platters will have you smiling 'til your next meal.

#dontjudgeabookbyitscover

CAPTAIN BOB
End of Saydet el Bihar, by the water,
behind Makbaret Sour

This famously popular seafront shack offers daily fish catches – best indulged with Arak or cold beer – under the amusing eye of chatty "Captain Bob".

#comedydining

CLOUD 59
Tyr public beach
Telephone: +961 (0)3 517996
Daily from 11am-2am

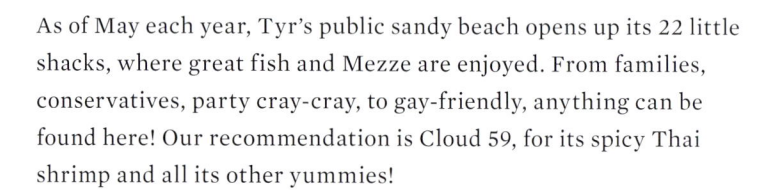

As of May each year, Tyr's public sandy beach opens up its 22 little shacks, where great fish and Mezze are enjoyed. From families, conservatives, party cray-cray, to gay-friendly, anything can be found here! Our recommendation is Cloud 59, for its spicy Thai shrimp and all its other yummies!

LE PHENICIEN
Old port, Tyr
Telephone: +961 7 740564
Daily from noon-12am

This charming seafood restaurant, right on the Tyr port, prepares delectable daily catches and specials that you won't find anywhere else in the country. This joint has been doing its thing for over 80 years now, and is the mother of Beirut's branch.

#fishisking #prawnisqueen

SNACKS

FURN EL-BAHR
Sahat et-Chouhada
Telephone: +961 7 740654
Daily from 7am-8pm

This modern bakery prepares heavenly traditional pastries. Big shout-out to them as, in terms of taste, this is where it's at when it comes to the "real" old- school Lebanon.

#respect

GUIDED TOURS

TASTE LEBANON
WWW.TASTELEBANON.CO.UK

For all you lazy motherfuckers, who enjoy your food, check these helpful cats out. Taste Lebanon organizes tailor-made culinary treks and experiences so that you can enjoy some authentic good food without having to worry about planning any of it! They also happen to be very cool people so don't be shy.

#butiamletired

CLUB GRAPPE
TELEPHONE: +961 70 432640 | CK@CLUBGRAPPE.COM
WWW.CLUBGRAPPE.COM

Feeling sluggish or simply overwhelmed by all the wine and Arak to be tasted? Get in touch with these guys, and they'll sort everything out for you from taking you out on a full day wine trip around the Bekaa Valley (starting price: 45$ /person), to wining and dining you or treating you to some cheese tasting (starting price: 40$ /person).

#lazy #doitforme

TIPS

★ OUR SUPERHERO ★

Prices Can be in Lebanese pounds or dollars, (1$=LBP 1.500). Don't be alarmed if you pay in dollars and receive your change in Lebanese pounds. The Lebanese like to mix them up.

Never drink tap water.

In case of an unfortunate 'traveller's belly', have a shot of undiluted *Arak*. I promise it works a treat!

Armenian food should always be accompanied by *Arak*.

In Lebanon, they tend to take your plate away as soon as you're done with your dish, even if others you're dining with are still digging into theirs. Deal with it.

In the meantime, please remember not to throw toilet paper in the loo, but in the bin, so as not to clog the toilet.

Waiters may also ask you "Khallas?" (pronounced Rrrallas) before taking your plate, which translates as "finished?".

Always check bills or menus to see if service charges are included in the price. The recommended amount is 10%. Some places can be quite sneaky about this!

If you find yourself in the unfortunate position of being in Beirut on a diet, swap the bread for white cabbage leaves and keep enjoying those dips!

Try to be understanding, don't lose patience and always remember that Lebanese service is far from flawless. Curiously, the service is usually outstanding in the authentic established restaurants and appalling in most eateries serving foreign cuisine.

Before leaving a typically Lebanese restaurant, be sure to tip the man who served you Lebanese coffee around LBP 5.000.

Lebanese restaurants serve rather big portions so be careful not to over order (even though the waiter will make sure that you do!)

MEAT THE FISH

OUR FAVOURITE POP-UP!
AND WE LIKED IT SO MUCH WE THINK IT DESERVES TWO WHOLE PAGES

Serving fresh products, Meat the Fish will deliver anything from yellowtail Hamachi, smoked swordfish, to Wagyu beef tenderloin to your door. Whether you'd like it raw to prepare yourself, or already cooked and seasoned, all services are available. Want to thank some local friends of yours for letting you crash at their place? Meat the Fish's beautiful gourmet gift baskets are the way to go! Check out their Facebook page as this bunch likes to pop-up around town and #occupy restaurants. Recommended order: oysters! (at 3$ a piece).

MEAT THE FISH TELEPHONE: +961 (0)5 531904

WWW.MEATTHEFISH.COM

INFO@MEATTHEFISH.COM

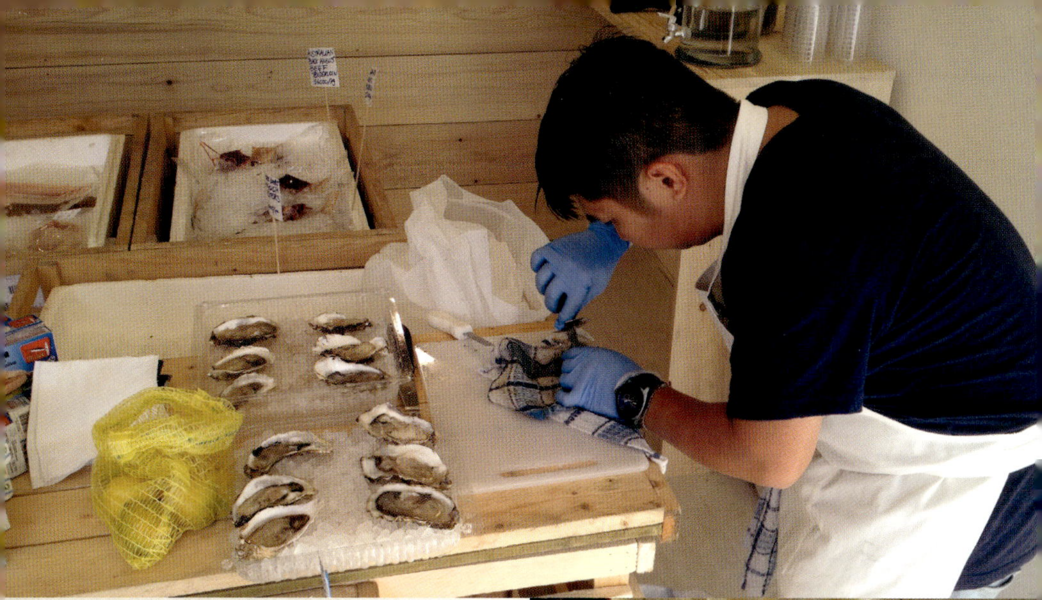

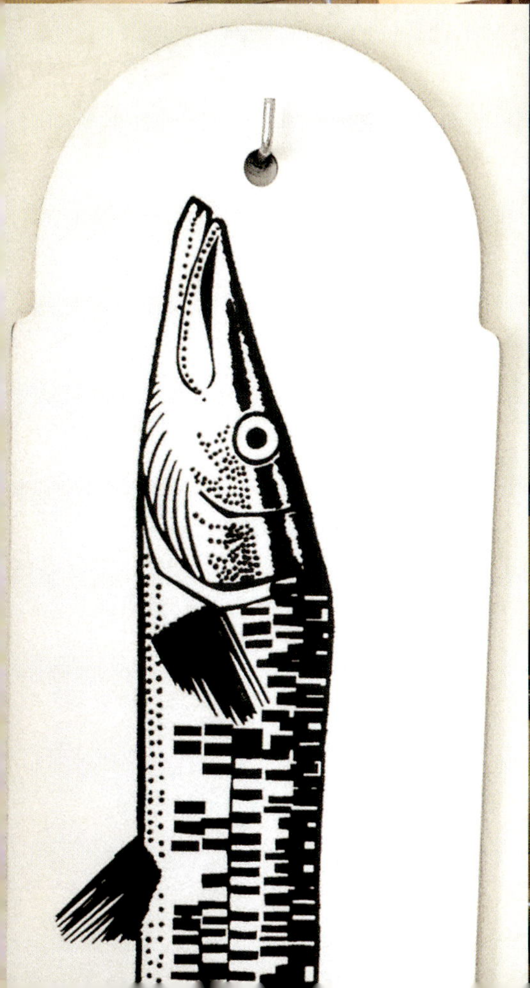

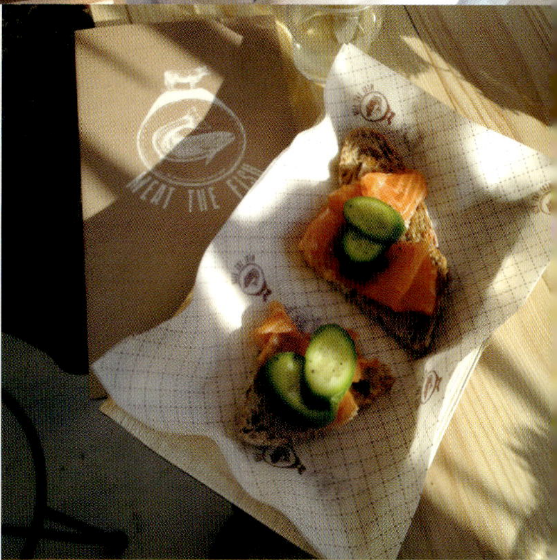
MEAT THE FISH

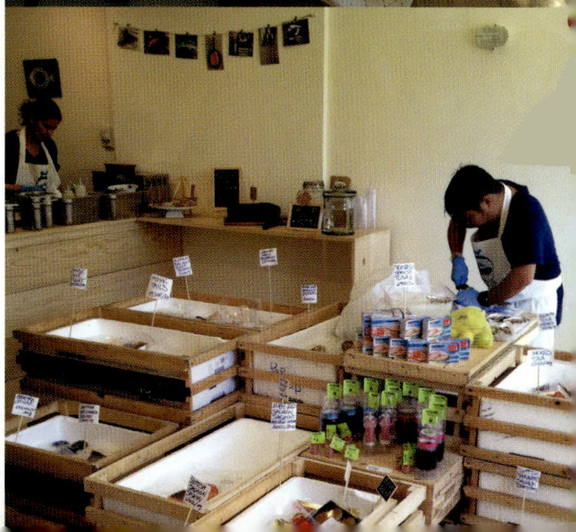

SAY WHAT?! SURVIVAL MENU

A rabic isn't exactly an easy language, we get it, and since we don't want you to miss out on some great dishes because you randomly pointed at French fries on the menu, we've created a survival menu glossary explaining what's what. All Arabic words have been phonetically translated into English, meaning that the spelling may differ but the pronunciation remains the same (minus our stinky accent). So where we write *Kishk*, others may write Kashk, Keshk, Kish, Kurt Qurut or even Qurt. Every italic word in the guide is also defined, making sure our readers don't get lost in translation.

SALADS

FATTOUSH: The traditionally peasant Lebanese salad, is a mix of fresh vegetables served with lemon dressing and topped with crisped bread. *Fattoush* or *Tabouleh*: an eternal dilemma when one ordering a Mezze – often solved by ordering both! *Fattoush* is in a way the peasant brother of *Tabouleh*; a salad of the garden's goodies, tomato, cucumber, radish, mint, green pepper, parsley... and grilled bread. The dressing can be as simple as *Sumac* and olive oil, and the grilled bread (some prefer it fried ... another dilemma), is added only at the last moment to keep it crunchy.

KHYAR BI LABAN: Cucumber and yoghurt salad.

SALATAT HUMMUS: Fresh chickpeas salad.

SALATAT ZAATAR AKHDAR: Green thyme salad.

TABOULEH: Following the original Lebanese recipe, this salad should be made with Burghul wheat (instead of couscous), finely chopped tomatoes, mint, onions and lots and lots of parsley, really lots of it... Seasoned with olive oil, lemon juice and salt.

SAMBUSAC: PASTRIES

FATAYER BI SABANIKH: Or the "spinach triangles" for those who are ashamed of their Arabic pronunciation. Just take a bite of these pastries filled with spinach, herbs and lemon.

KELLAGE: Some people call them the Lebanese quesadillas. But let's not compare Lebanon to Mexico. A pastry crust filled with cheese. Usually *Halloumi* cheese.

LAHM BI AJEEN: Litteraly means meat with pastry. Round flat bread topped with ground lamb meat, onions and tomatoes. Also known as the Lebanese mini pizza, you can choose different toppings (just like pizza).

LAHMACUN: Thin baked bread topped with minced meat, vegetables and herbs, and seasoned with lemon.

MANOUCHE JIBNE: A big round flat bread topped with

cheese (*Jibne* or *Akkawi* cheese).

MANOUCHE ZA'ATAR: Round flat bread topped with thyme, olive oil, Sumac and sesame seeds. Also a big favourite for breakfast (see p.10).

RKAKAT JIBNE: Filo pastry rolls filled with *Jibne* cheese then fried.

SAMBOUSEK BI JIBNE: Triangular pastries (comparable to samosas or empanadas, but not really) filled with *Jibne* or *Akkawi* cheese.

SAMBOUSEK LAHME: Triangular pastries filled with lamb and pine nuts.

SFIHA: The exact same recipe as *Lahm bi Ajeen*, but looks more like a little square lamb chausson.

MEZZE: STARTERS

ARAYES KAFTA: Grilled grounded lamb mixed with herbs and onions in warm flat bread, served with yoghurt.

ARNABEET MEKLI: Deep fried cauliflower.

BATATA BIL KIZBARA: Fried potatoes with coriander.

BASTERMA: Heavily seasoned, air-dried cured beef of Anatolian origin. It is prepared by salting the meat, then washing it with water and letting it dry for 10–15 days. It is usually served in thin slices, usually uncooked, but sometimes lightly grilled or added to eggs for breakfast. It may be added to different dishes, the most famous of which is a bean dish, (Yakhnet Fasoulia w Rizz b Basturma), and various pies.

BATHINJAN MEKLI: Fried aubergines in oil with fresh lemon juice.

BATHINJAN MOUTABAL OR BABA GHANNOUJ: Aubergine dip mixed with *Tahini* and lemon, topped with extra virgin olive.

BAYD W AWARMA: Fried or scrambled eggs with warm minced lamb (or beef), caramelized onion and garlic.

FALAFEL: Deep fried balls made with chickpeas and/or fava beans. Served with *Tahini* and tomatoes.

FOUL: Mashed fava beans served with olive oil, chopped parsley, onions, garlic and lemon juice.

HALLOUMI: Semi-hard cheese made from a mixture of goat's and sheep's milk. Originally from Cyprus, it is served grilled or fried.

HINDBEH BIL ZAYT: Sautéed dandelion leaves in olive oil with garlic, parsley, and caramelized onions.

HUMMUS: The word itself means "chickpea", and the exact term for the famous dip would be *Hummus bi Tahini*. Cooked and crushed chickpeas mixed with *Tahini*, lemon and garlic. It is said that you can judge a restaurant by its *Hummus*. So easy to prepare but harder to get just right.

HUMMUS AWARMA: *Hummus* toped with warm minced lamb (or beef) caramelized onion and garlic give.

HUMMUS BALILA: A hot dip of mashed chickpeas, cumin, and toasted pine nuts.

KIBBEH AKRAS: Fried balls of ground meat and *Burghul*, stuffed with minced meat, onions and pine nuts. Lebanon's national dish!

KIBBEH NAYYE: Or raw *Kibbeh*, consists of minced raw lamb or beef mixed with fine *Burghul* and spices.

LABNEH: Strained yoghurt topped with extra virgin olive oil. Also eaten at breakfast.

LOUBYA BI ZAYT: Green beans, tomatoes and onions cooked in oil.

MAQANEQ: Tiny lamb sausages flambéed in olive oil and lemon.

MOUHAMMARA: Sweet spicy red pepper paste with crushed walnuts, used as a dip or to flavour food.

MSABBAHA: A variation of *Hummus*, where some chickpeas remain whole.

NIKHAAT: Fried lamb brains. For the most adventurous.

SHANKLISH: Dried cheese, covered with thyme and sometimes hot pepper too. Shanklish is part of the Mouneh (see p.12), and can be conserved for a year. It is not consumed as a cheese, but always served as a salad with tomato, onion and olive oil.

SOUJOK: Spicy sausages with mixed beef and lamb meat.

WARAK ENAB BI ZAYT: In Lebanon, there are two popular versions of this vine leaf staple: a vegetarian recipe - vine leaves stuffed with rice, vegetables and spices - and a recipe that includes ground beef in the vine leaf stuffing as well as lamb shanks in the cooking pot. They can also be served alone as a full meal.

CHICKEN DISHES

FARROUJ MESHWI: Deboned half chicken marinated in lemon juice, garlic and olive oil, then grilled. If you like garlic, you will love this dish.

JAWANEH: Chicken wings marinated in garlic and lemon.

RIZ MAA DJEJ: Chicken, rice, herbs and pine nuts. Simply yummy.

SHAWARMA DJEJ: *Shawarma* is the Lebanese term for *Kebab*. This marinated chicken dish is mixed with spices and cut in thin slices. Although it can be served on a plate (generally with accompaniments), *Shawarma* also refers to a flat bread sandwich or wrap made with *Shawarma* meat and *Tahini* sauce.

SHISH TAOUK: Cubes of chicken that are marinated, then skewered and grilled. Common marinades are based upon yogurt and lemon juice or tomato puree, though there are many variations. *Shish Taouk* is typically eaten with *Toum*.

MANSAF DJEJ: Mansaf means explosion in Arabic. Chicken served with yogurt sauce.

MEAT DISHES

ARDICHOWKE BI LAHME: Artichoke stuffed with lamb meat and yoghurt and garnished with pine nuts.

BAZELLA MAA RIZ: Pea stew with rice, carrots and small cubes of beef.

DAOUD BACHA: Meat balls with rice, onions and a tomato sauce. Fattet Bathinjan: Aubergine with yoghurt, minced meat, herbs and pine nuts.

FRAKEH: Raw lamb or veal mixed with Burghul, onions and herbs.

KAFTA BIL SANIEH: Ground meat baked in a pan, served with potatoes and tomato sauce.

KOFTA MEKLI: Fried lamb or beef fingers.

KOFTA MESHWI: Grilled lamb or beef fingers.

KEBAB: Or *Shawarma*, it refers to meat that is cooked over or next to flames; large or small cuts of meat, or even ground meat; it may be served on plates, in sandwiches, or in bowls. The traditional meats for *Kebab* in Lebanon are lamb and chicken.

KIBBEH BI LABAN: Fried balls of ground meat and *Bulghur*, stuffed with minced meat, onions and pine nuts (*Kibbeh*) in yoghurt.

KIBBEH BIL SANIEH: Same recipe as *Kibbeh Akras* but fried in a flat oven plate, which gives it a flat shape.

KHARUF MEHSHI: Roasted lamb stuffed with rice and almonds.

KOUSSA MEHSHI: Courgette stuffed with lamb and rice.

LABAN OMOU: Cubes of boiled lamb simmered in yoghurt and flavoured with garlic and coriander.

MAAKARONA BIL SANIEH: Spaghetti with meat, sprinkled with grated cheese, and baked in the pan.

MALFOUF MAHSHI: Cabbage leaves stuffed with lamb and rice.

MANTI: Crunchy meat ravioli covered in a garlic yoghurt sauce.

QAWARMA: Seasoned minced lamb and pine nuts served in a variety of ways (on top of *Hummus*, on a *Manouche* etc...).

SHISH BARAK: Tiny meat dumplings cooked in a yoghurt stew.

FISH DISHES

SAMAK BI TAHINI: Baked fish (usually Sea Bass, Cod, Hake or Grouper) with *Tahini* sauce.

SAMAK MESHWI: Or fish *Kebab*. Whole pan grilled fresh Mediterranean fish, served with *Taratour* or *Tahini*.

SAMKE HARRA: Marinated fish, grilled and topped with a lightly spiced sauce.

SAYADIYEH: Lebanese baked fish with rice and fried onions.

VEGETARIAN DISHES

BEMIEH BI ZAYT: Okra dish flavoured with garlic and coriander.

FASSOLIA BI RIZ: Hot bean stew with rice.

FATTEH HUMMUS: Toasted pieces of flat bread croutons mixed with *Tahini*, yoghurt and *Hummus*.

MAKHLOUTA: Lentil soup with beans and rice (*Makhlouta* means « mixture » in Lebanese).

MJADDARA OR MOUDARDARA: Cooked lentils together with groats, rice, and garnished with sautéed onions.

MUSAQA: Aubergine and chickpea stew with pomegranate.

YAKHNET BATATA: Potato stew.

YAKHNET SABANIKH: Spinach stew. Served with rice and lemon.

BREAD

FURN: Term used nowadays for Arabic bread made commercially. It also used to be the village bakery.

KAAK: Just in case Lebanese food wasn't complicated enough, here you have a half-bread half-dessert goodie, that looks like a purse. Flat and round with a hole in the middle and covered with sesame seeds, this street bread is best found sold by street vendors. Fill it with salty stuff (meat, cheese, *Hummu*s, *Labneh*) or sweet stuff (*Knefe*, dates, sweet walnuts and pistachios). *Kaak* also means "cake" in Arabic.

KHUBZ ARABI OR KMAJ: Better known as Pita, this leavened wheat bread, is either round or oval, and of variable size. Flatbread in general, whether leavened or not, is among the most ancient of breads. In the Arabic world, Pita is a foreign word, all breads are called *Khubz* (meaning bread), and specifically this bread is known as *Khubz arabi* (Arabic bread).

MARKOUK OR SAJ: Another flatbread, but this time super flat. It is baked on a domed or convex metal griddle, also known as *Saj*. It is usually larger than *Khubz*, and thinner, almost translucent.

TLAMI: Round, soft-textured, thick bread.

DESSERTS

AREESH: Cheese made from slowly heated yogurt until it curdles and separates, then placed in cheesecloth to drain. It is similar in taste to Ricotta. Served with Honey.

ASMALIYAH: Two layers of roasted vermicelli are filled with cream. It is served with sugar syrup.

AWAMAT: Crisp fried syrupy doughnut balls.

BAKLAWA: Assorted nuts-and-syrup-soaked Mediterranean pastry dessert.

BARAZEK: Crunchy, nutty, lightly sweet honey and sesame seeds cookies.

BOUZA BI HALEEB: Milk ice cream with pistachios sprinkled on top.

CHAABIYAT: Filo dough cakes with orange cream and pistachio filling, drizzled in syrup.

HALAWA: Flaky sweet confection based on crushed sesame seeds with pistachios.

KNEFE: Hot pastry with sweet *Akkawi* cheese inside. Also common for breakfast.

MAAMOUL: Semolina-based pastries filled with fresh dates, walnuts or pistachios.

LOUKOUM: A family of confections based on a gel of starch and sugar. Premium varieties consist largely of chopped dates, pistachios, and hazelnuts or walnuts bound by the gel; traditional varieties are mostly gel, generally flavoured with rosewater, mastic, Bergamot orange, or lemon. The confection is often packaged and eaten in small cubes dusted with icing sugar, copra, or powdered cream of tartar, to prevent clinging.

MAAKROUN: Sweet fried semolina, orange blossom water and walnut cake.

MEGHLI: Floured rice pudding served to well wishers when a baby is born. Very popular during Christmas.

MOUFATAKA: Rice pudding with *Tahini*, turmeric and pine nuts.

MOUHALABIEH: Firm and milky pudding, topped with orange blossom jam and pistachio.

MOUWARAKA: Gold and crispy spirals filled with sugar,

almonds, cinnamon, walnuts and orange blossom water!

NAMOURA: Semolina cake soaked in syrup, decorated with almonds.

RIZ BEL HALIB: Rice pudding.

SFOUF: Spongy, eggless almond-semolina cake served with tea or milk.

SIMSMIYEH: Sesame nougat.

TAHINOV HATS: Sweet Armenian bread roll with Tahini, sugar and cinnamon.

TAMRIYEH: Grounded semolina, orange blossom water and sugar.

DRINKS

AL QAHWAH: Arabic or Turkish coffee. Roasted and then finely ground coffee beans are boiled in a pot, but brewed without adding sugar. Cardamom is often added, or served plain, but no cream or milk.

AHWEH BAYDA: Literally meaning "white coffee", this drink has nothing to do with coffee other than in name. The caffeine-free drink is made from water, orange blossom water, and can be sweetened with sugar, if you're in need of a serious sugar rush. It is traditionally thought to facilitate digestion and soothe the nerves.

AMAR EL DIN: Just like drinking apricots. Imagine a dried apricot paste, soaked in water and boiled for a short while to obtain a silky thick liquid, of an apricot colour. This drink is then scented with orange blossom water and rose water, and served fresh. The *Amar el din* is a "must" for Iftaar. This velvety, soft and sweet drink is perfect on an empty stomach.

ARAK: One of the Lebanese culinary symbols. Usually served with Mezze, the word *Arak* means "sweat". This alcoholic beverage (40–63%), scented with aniseed, is served diluted with water (usually one part *Arak* to two parts water) and with a lot of ice. *Arak* is not only a drink, but a way of life, a ritual, a style of eating and drinking for hours and hours.

JELLAB: Drink made from grape molasses and raisins mixed together and topped with pine nuts.

LABAN AYRAN: A cold minted yoghurt drink mixed with salt.

LIMONADA: Drink of lemon juice and sugar.

SAHLAB: Once considered an aphrodisiac drink, true *Sahlab* is now becoming rarer. *Sahlab*, based on an increasingly rare orchid, is a popular winter drink all over the Levant, like hot almond milk. The tubers of Orchis macula are boiled, dried, and then ground to a grey powder that makes a creamy drink when cooked in milk.

SHARAB EL TOUT: Mulberry syrup often served cold to welcome guest with a fresh and tasty drink.

SHARAB EL WARED: Rose water syrup often served cold to guests when tea or coffee are not desired.

INGREDIENTS

AKKAWI OR JIBNE: White semi-hard cheese that melts well when heated. Used most often for sweet pastries.

AJEEN: Pastry dough required in many of the dishes that can be either used directly or frozen in a plastic bag for later use.

BURGHUL: "Glory to the rice, and *Burghul* hung itself " says an old proverb. Which means that the *Burghul*, this original old ingredient, lost its importance in the face of imported rice. *Burghul* or bread, are the necessary cereals of every meal. It is prepared from wheat, washed, cleaned and steamed, before being dried, then ground to different thickness: big, to cook like rice, fine, for the *Tabouleh*, or very fine, for preparations like *Kibbeh*.

DARFIYEH: Raw goat's milk and fermented in goat's skin.

FOUL MAACHOUR: Large pods of fava beans that have been stripped of their skin and split, used to prepare *Falafel*.

FREEKEH: A cereal food made from green wheat that goes through a roasting process in its production.

GHEE: A class of clarified butter used to cook *Knefe*.

KABISS: Almost all the garden's vegetables are preserved in jars as *Kabiss* (pickles), or vegetables preserved in brine: cucumbers, aubergines, turnips, cabbages, etc. There is a powerful preoccupation with food conservation, and preserving the best of summer for the cold days of winter. Some vegetables are preserved in brine, salt and water, others in vinegar and brine, and others in olive oil. *Kabiss* is served as appetizer or accompaniment of certain dishes, like the *Falafel* and *Shawarma*.

KASHTA: Form of clotted cream made by skimming boiling milk, used in many of the Lebanese desserts.

KISHK: A mixture of both cereals (*Burghul*) and dairy (*Laban*). It is a clever way to transform and preserve these two indispensable ingredients for the cold days of the winter. After fermentation, the mixture is dried in the sun, and then rubbed to obtain a fine powder. *Kishk*, as a dried powder, can last for a year or more, and will be diluted in water to prepare soups or other dishes in winter.

KHISHNAH: Rice with vermicelli.

LABAN: Gave Lebanon its name – *Laban* for yogurt and "Loubnan" for Lebanon, as in the white snow covered mountains. Typical product of the Balkans and the eastern Mediterranean, *Laban* is eaten with bread, in salads and even cooked in stews – but never sweet or with fruits.

QATR: Sweet, flavoured syrup usually poured while very hot over pastries.

SUMAC: A typical ingredient from the mountains, essential for the Mouneh (see p.12). *Sumac* is a dark red powder with a particular lemony taste and is extracted from a wild shrub, which grows in medium height mountains. At the end of each branch grows a bouquet of tightened grains, like grapes or lentils, covered by a dark red skin. The grapes are shelled, the seeds dried in the shade, then ground, to extract the dark red cover. *Sumac* is a traditional substitute for lemon, and a basic ingredient in many dishes, such as *Fattoush* and eggs with *Sumac*.

TAHINI: Is not sesame oil, but sesame paste, made out of mashed seeds. *Tahini* is the sauce which accompanies many dishes, and is used as a basis for the *Tarator*, with lemon juice, salt and garlic. *Tahini* necessarily accompanies *Hummus bi Tahini*, the *Baba Ghanouj*, *Falafel*, *Shawarma* and is also used as a cooking sauce for meat and always served as a side with fish.

TARATOR: Sesame paste sauce to be used with *Shawarma*, *Falafel*, *Kofta* or over vegetables and fish.

TOUM: Garlic sauce with salt, olive oil and lemon juice.

OSMALLIYEH: Roasted vermicelli.

ZA'ATAR: A mix of dried thyme herbs, *Sumac* and sesame seeds.

FREE TRANSLATOR

"Bon Appétit"	Sahtein
Cheers	Kessak (for a guy)
	Kessek (for a girl)
	Kesskon (for a party!)
Dig in	Tfadal (for a guy)
	Tfadali (for a girl)
Very good	Kteer tayyeb
Enough	Rralass
Take-away	Take-away
Menu	Menu
Wine list	"Carte des vins"
The bill	El ehseb
How much?	Adesh?
Dessert	Hillo
Coffee	Ahweh
Without sugar	Bala sukar
I'm a vegetarian	Ana nabété (for a guy)
	Ana nabétiyyé (for a girl)
Please	Iza betreed

Thank you	Choukran
Yes	Eh
No	Lah
Toilets	Hamam
Waiter	"Maitre"
Water	My
Sal	Meleh
Pepper	Bhar
Napkin	Kleenex
Glass	Kebbeye
Plate	Sahen
Fork	Showkeh
Knife	Sekineh
Spoon	Mala'
Breakfast	Terwi-eh
Lunch	Rrad
Dinner	Asha

RECIPES

COLETTE KAHIL
OWNER OF BEIT EL BATROUN - BED & BREAKFAST

Q *What defines your cooking?*

A I love forgotten recipes from the mountains. I cook with what I have, blend things and improvise. I enjoy using the vegetables from my vegetable garden. At first I learnt from my elders and cookbooks - now I just invent and therefore never do the exact same thing twice.

Q *What would you choose as your last meal?*
A Burghul bel-banadoora, (*Burghul* and tomato pilaf).
It has an earthy taste and is the meal of the poor - my own recipe of the dish includes aubergine in it. I love it. For dessert: ice cream. I'm actually learning how to make it myself soon. I love mcetkh (Arabic gum) and chocolate flavours.

Q *What's your favourite ingredient/spice or herb?*
A Ground Pepper. I love its smell - it transports me straight away. Otherwise, fresh herbs, including basil and *Za'atar*. I am not that into meat or fish (only make it really for my kids, or others) I prefer vegetables.

Q *Any tips for beginners in Lebanese cooking?*
A Just go for it! It's not that difficult, and what is difficult or takes time, I don't even do. The vine leaves for example, I don't like preparing them as they take so long to do. I prefer making five dishes for a group, then taking too much time making one dish.

ARAK CAKE

For the cake:
- 5 eggs
- One teaspoon of vanilla
- Zest of one lemon
- One cup of sugar
- One cup of flour
- One cup of coconut powder
- 250gr of butter
- Two teaspoons of baking powder

How to:
1. Beat the eggs with the sugar
2. Mix in: a. Vanilla and lemon zest b. Melted butter c. Flour, baking powder and coconut
3. Place in 170C pre-heated oven until cooked

For the Syrup:
- One and half cups of sugar
- One cup of water
- A few drops of lemon juice
- One cup of Arak

How to:
1. Bring the sugar, water and lemon juice to boil and cook until it thickens into a syrupy texture
2. Remove from heat and let cool until warm
3. Add the Arak and mix
4. Once cake is cooked, remove from oven and pour syrup over it straight away

BEETROOT BIT HINI (OR BEETROOT HUMMUS)

Ingredients:
- 2 medium sized beetroots peeled, boiled until tender, and chopped
- 5 tbs of lemon juice (may need more/less depends on taste)
- 2 crushed cloves of garlic
- 4 tbs of water
- 1 ½ tbs of *Tahini*
- 1 tbs of yogurt
- Salt to taste

How to:

1. Combine beetroot, lemon juice, garlic, salt, *Tahini*, yogurt and water in a blender and blend roughly (you want it smooth but with some pieces)
2. Add more lemon, garlic or salt to taste

MAQLOUBEH BATENJAN
(OR TURNOVER AUBERGINE CASSEROLE)

Ingredients:

- 1/2 kg of beef, cut in cubes
- 2 large aubergines cut in large cubes
- 1 chopped onion
- 2 cups of Italian rice
- 7 spices-mix

How to:

1. Fry the meat cubes with the chopped onion in a large deep pan. Add salt and 7 spices, cover with water and cook
2. Deep fry the aubergine cubes and place them on kitchen towels to absorb excess oil
3. Add the cooked aubergines to the pan and simmer for 10 minutes
4. Strain all the water from the pan and use it to cook the rice in a separate pot: 1 cup of water for 1 cup of rice
5. When the rice is cooked through, add it to the pan on top of the aubergine and meat. Carefully pat down the rice to form a solid top layer
6. Tip the pan over unto a large flat serving dish, being careful not to break up the layers
7. Serve with yoghurt or a side salad

SARKIS AKELIAN
AKA SAKO-BARTENDER AT EPICERY

Q *What drink do you order when you hit the bars?*
A Any of the classics.

Q *If you had to choose one drink for the rest of your life?*
A Red wine.

Q *Cocktail you hate making?*
A Sangria.

Q *Best cure for a hangover?*
A Have the same drink you had the previous night.

TWISTED COSMO

1. Coat the glass with *Arak*
2. In a shaker: mix 1 cl fresh lime juice, 1cl orange curaçao, 3cl vodka, 3cl cranberry juice, 2 drops of lime bitter and 2cl home-made thyme syrup
3. Garnish with orange zest and fresh Lebanese wild thyme.
4. (To make thyme syrup: 1L water, 1000g of sugar, 4 specks of thyme
5. Bring to the boil, then turn heat off, cover and let it sit for 30 minutes)

APPLE TEQUILA CIDER

1. Add ¼ mashed fresh apple, with 1 cl lime juice, 1cl homemade cinnamon syrup, 1cl simple syrup, 2 cl tequila white, 4cl apple sour liquor, 2 drop of cardamom bitter, and 1 dash of *Arak* to top it off
2. To make cinnamon syrup: 1L water, 1000g of sugar, 4 cinnamon sticks. Bring to the boil, then turn heat off, cover and let it sit for 1 hour

THE FOOD GUIDE: BEIRUT ON A PLATE

ABOUT THE AUTHORS

Leonore and Olivia Dicker are two sisters who have a deep, passionate and unconditional love for food. Raised in cosmopolitan London by a German father and a French mother, they now spend most of their time daydreaming about their next meal as they try out new restaurants and recipes. Travelling is their second big passion as it enables them to discover new cultures and ... new culinary experiences.

Leonore is a journalist who has worked in vibrant cities around the world, such as New York and Paris – and more developing ones like Astana. Her curiosity prompted her to write for a variety of sectors including travel (Time Out Beirut), fashion (ELLE), business (World Investment News) and lifestyle (Paris Match). That is until she found The One: food. She currently resides in Beirut.

Olivia has a background in the contemporary art market. Having both studied and worked in Paris, she decided to discover the world while pursuing her career. She left her beloved *vin et fromage* to taste other delights from other countries, such as Germany and China.